Growing In Faith

Growing In Faith

A True Bronner Story

By

Lorene Bronner

ISBN-13: 978-1986842655
ISBN-10: 1986842657

DEDICATION TO MY FAMILY

The gifts I would give you are not something that you can see or hold in your hands.
I give you love from my heart.
I give you time, so that we can share our thoughts and express whatever is going on.
I give you spiritual advice that comes from God.
I give you hugs and kisses from breast to breast and heart to heart.
I give you thanks for all that you do for me, the sharing, caring for me when I am well or ill.
I give you thanks for taking me on trips with you and sending me on a trip with my friend.
I give you thanks for the good food that you cook.
I give you thanks for caring, sharing and supporting each other.
But most of all, I give you love.
I thank God for blessing me with seven beautiful daughters (one deceased), eight handsome grandsons (two deceased), one beautiful granddaughter and three beautiful great-granddaughters.
I thank God for allowing me to live this many years (83) with His grace and mercy.
The best things in life are free.

PREFACE

This true story is a testament to the goodness of God and how He brought me from a life of sin to redemption and peace. My story tells about the mental and physical abuse I suffered for approximately thirteen of the twenty-three years of marriage to the father of my children. It tells how pride had a devastating effect on my wellbeing.

At the time I did not recognize what it was because I had never seen it exemplified in my upbringing. Because of my parents' and grandparents' loving relationships, I was ignorant as to what people can do to each other in a so-called loving relationship. Getting punched in the face for having a conversation with a male customer in our place of business gave me instant confirmation of what physical abuse is. It took a little longer for me to recognize the mental abuse.

I am grateful to God for allowing me to live and experience life at eighty-three years of age. Many years of my life have been spent agonizing over my past and all the foolish mistakes I made, and the choices that I allowed myself to make because of jealousy, revenge and an unforgiving heart. My past has been repeated over and over in my head and has caused so much indescribable pain.

I have prayed to God to release me from this pain. What I came to realize was that I had to repent, admit my sin, stop blaming others, and take responsibility for my own unwise decisions. Of course, I was influenced in many instances, but it was my decision to go along or not.

I want to share who I am with my children, grandchildren, great- grands and others. My motivation comes from a great spiritual desire to share how God has worked in my life and provided all my needs, and how He positioned the right people in my life at my time of need. This is a true testimony of God's grace and mercy as it relates to my life as a child, adult, wife, mother, widow, grandmother and great-grandmother.

Carrying anger, resentment, bitterness and pain for many years has been a terrible burden to bear. Living past hurts over and over in my head has been like being on constant punishment. Writing my story has brought some relief, but it was just the beginning of a long process of healing, as readers of this story will realize.

I hope this book will help someone who is in a similar situation to be able to identify what abuse looks like, whether physical or mental. If this effort can help one person, I will be grateful. In my life experiences, whenever I decide to do something positive, negativity starts to work immediately. Negative thoughts come pouring in, e.g.: "How are you going to write a book? You are not a writer. You are not famous. Who would want to read your book? Who will publish it?"

This scripture keeps me grounded:

Isaiah 54:17 No weapon formed against me shall prosper, And every tongue which rises against me in judgment I shall condemn. (KJV)

ACKNOWLEDGEMENTS

I feel hopelessly inadequate to express my gratitude to the many people who have encouraged and prayed with and for me on this journey of writing my story. I thank God for allowing me to live long enough to get it finished. Many of the people involved in my book when I started writing, have transitioned. I feel much sadness that they will not have the opportunity to read my story.

Thanks to my sister and best friend, Claudia Munford-Robinson, for sharing and caring for me and setting great examples to follow. I attended many of her Bible studies at Mount Airy Presbyterian Church, Germantown Avenue and Mount Pleasant Streets in Philadelphia. I attended Bible retreats that she was involved in for many years.

By the influence of my own children, I am continually learning and growing in the word of God. My daughter Deanne Bronner-Hale has a Bible study in her home, assisted by Minister Phyllis Pryor. Deanne also ministers to her clients at her Collage Beauty Salon at 6813 Germantown Avenue, Philadelphia, PA 19119. She will pray for you whether you want your hair done or not.

Thanks to my youngest daughter, Sonja J. Bronner, for praying and discussing Bible scriptures with me once a week. Sonja took over a Bible study during her six-month deployment to Camp Lemonier, Djibouti, Africa. Upon returning home she started a Bible class in her home.

I probably would not have finished this book without the help of my daughter, Dr. Tauheedah Bronner, who spent countless hours proofreading and making corrections, helping with my computer skills and always encouraging me to continue to write.

To Deborah, Linda and Kala, your concern and loving support is appreciated to the highest degree. You have always been available when I needed helping hands.

To my Pastor, Rev. K. Marshall Williams Sr., at the Nazarene Baptist Church on Germantown Avenue in Philadelphia, for being a Bible teaching minister and encouraging us to study the Bible every day. Through his messages I have learned many scriptures and have read the entire Bible (KJV) three times. Our First Lady, Sister Connie Williams, leads a prayer ministry that is outstanding and far-reaching to other churches in and outside of our community. I have been blessed to be a part of this ministry.

To the King David Lodge #52 members and the widows of the same lodge, your words of encouragement have always helped when I needed it the most.

To my grandson Tyrone Appling for suggesting the title of my book before I had the first chapter written.

To my cousin Vincent T. Williams, President and CEO of Williams Group, Inc., author of "How Do I Reach My True Destiny?" Many times, when I had put my book aside, you would call and get me back on track. I am grateful for your support.

By participating in Sunday School classes at Nazarene Church taught by Rev. Dunn, Rev. Ora Love's ministry "Church Without Walls", and Pastor Mary Roberson's Conference Bible Study, I have grown to a higher faith level that has enhanced my life to a greater degree than I can explain. The title of my book was confirmed during our Bible study.

INTRODUCTION

My story is a personal journey of emotional extremes that began in a difficult period of American History. Migrating from the Deep South of Alabama, where my mother died from a tooth extraction at the age of 25 (more than likely because of improper treatment in a segregated ward hospital), to my life in the North, where I met and married the love of my life.

Unconditional love for my husband produced seven daughters, one deceased shortly after birth. It was a marriage that started in the highest state of euphoria and turned into a chaotic disaster of mental and physical abuse, jealousy, secrets and lies and an unsolved cold case murder.

All the tests, trials, and tribulations that I experienced taught me to seek a closer relationship with God. Reading and researching His word gave me a higher level of growth in my faith and created a relationship with God that I never experienced before. Because of God's love and compassion for His children, I am blessed.

I surrendered my life to Christ at the age of eleven but did not understand what to do next. Studying God's word daily has been the answer for me. Time spent studying and meditating on His word brings peace and joy that is indescribable. I am a work in progress: "Growing in Faith."

TABLE OF CONTENTS

CHAPTER ONE

My Beginning

It was right in the middle of the great depression when I was born, in May of 1934, Gosport, Alabama. This was a crucial time in the history of the United States, before the start of World War II (1939-1945). It was a time when many Alabamians suffered financial setbacks. After the start of World War I, jobs were available in the shipbuilding industry in Mobile. My father and some of my family members worked at the shipyard. Alabama farmers, like my grandfather, increased production of cotton and food to meet the needs of the times.

Whenever I was asked where I was born, I used to say "Mobile" as a reference point because if you weren't born in Gosport, chances are you had not heard of it. It is located about one hundred miles south of Mobile, between Jackson and Claiborne.

Gosport's population was about 99% black and everyone knew each other. I think we were also related to almost everyone who lived there. There was a sense of community that was unparalleled; parents were parents to all the children. If you were caught doing wrong by an adult your parents would be told and there would be consequences. I would not classify it as a town, but a stopover on the way to town.

One area was named 'Nigger Town'. No whites ever lived there but there were plantations controlled by overseers. This place called Gosport was unique in every way imaginable, completely segregated, very few white people, no post office, and a one-room schoolhouse that had removable partitions to separate the classes when school was in session. The school went as high as the eighth grade.

The few white children that lived in Gosport were bused to Grove Hill, to the segregated white school. There were three churches that blacks attended in the area and three stores, two were white owned and my grandfather, Luviger Denson, owned the third. Some of the black people in Gosport were sharecroppers but most owned their homes and many acres of land.

In some areas, when it rained hard enough to make the creeks rise, the people who lived on the other side of the creek could not get to school or leave their homes for fear of drowning in the creek. There were no bridges and you had to walk across the creek on a big log that was wide enough that a person would not easily fall off. It could be intimidating if you were not used to walking on logs. "If the Lord spare me and the creek don't rise I'll see you tomorrow", was a parting statement used by many who lived on the other side of the creek.

I was blessed to be born the second child of Maggie D. Denson-Morris and Willie D. Morris, a loving couple who married at an early age (fifteen and seventeen) and became the parents to me, Lorene Morris, my older sister Claudia D. Morris and my younger brother Luviger Morris. My parents lived with my grandfather, Luviger Denson, affectionately called Big Daddy, and his wife, Carrie, who we called MaMa. We were born with the help of a midwife inside the house that my grandfather Big Daddy built.

I do not have a vivid memory of MaMa Carrie. I remember her being soft-spoken and very kind with generous hugs and kisses. MaMa became ill with a disease of the kidneys in 1941 and passed away at the age of 40.

18

I don't have knowledge of how long MaMa and Big Daddy were married. My mother was their only child. I was maybe six or seven years old when MaMa passed. I remember them having her in the living room of the house in a casket and people being there all night. It was called a wake. A family member held me up to the casket and tried to coerce me into kissing my grandmother. I screamed and hollered until the person put me down. I was so afraid of dead people until I could not sleep that night because of frightening dreams about them.

Eventually, my mother and father were able to move to Florida where my father had a job working as a supervisor on a large farm owned by a white man. Everything was going well for him for a short time until a co-worker who was also white and did not like it that my father was his boss, threatened him. He told my father that he had better leave or he would be sorry. Therefore, for fear of harm being done to his wife and children, my father left and came back to Gosport to my grandfather's house.

After that period my mother and father moved to Mobile and my father was drafted into the Army. That was in 1942. Daddy was employed at the shipyard at the time and was making a good salary. This was a great period in our lives, living in Mobile in a new housing development on Conception Street. We enjoyed going to a school where the quality of education was much higher than in Gosport.

My mother was beautiful and talented. She had a gift of sewing. She made all our dresses and dressed my sister and me alike. We also looked alike so, people thought we were twins. People told me that I looked like my mother and how pretty I was, and that did not help me. I started to think I was better than most and developed a selfish and judgmental attitude. I would pick other people apart without knowing them and have an opinion from the moment I would meet them.

Questions and thoughts, usually negative, would come flowing into my mind. "What is wrong with him or her? Who does she think she is? She looks horrible with that ugly dress." These were thoughts that invaded my mind and gave me a sense of superiority. Many years passed before I recognized this very bad flaw in my personality. It has caused me much pain in my adulthood.

Proverbs 31:10-13 Who can find a virtuous wife? For her worth is far above rubies. The heart of her husband safely trusts her; So, he will have no lack of gain. She does him good and not evil All the days of her life. She seeks wool and flax, And willingly works with her hands. (KJV)

We made new friends in Mobile and felt safe and secure with our mom and dad. My mother was the epitome of a virtuous woman. She was an excellent housekeeper, cleanliness reigned supreme, everything had a place, and everything was kept in its place. She provided good meals and showered us with lots of love. My father was handsome and debonair. He was a good provider and treated my mother with respect and love. They set good examples for us to follow. Our home was peaceful, and we felt very safe and loved.

During the summer months my sister, brother and I would go back to Gosport and spend time with our grandfather Big Daddy and grandmother MaMa before she passed. Working on the farm during those periods was like a retreat vacation and we loved it.

Three years after MaMa passed, while my father was during his tour of duty, my mother became ill. My mother had a tooth pulled and developed lockjaw. She was hospitalized in the Mobile Infirmary in Mobile, Alabama. I believe she had mitral valve prolapse. I was diagnosed with the condition in my forties, and each time I go to the dentist I am instructed to take penicillin before I go as a precaution to prevent such a thing from happening.

During this time discrimination and segregation were rampant, and my mother was treated at a segregated hospital. She was not treated promptly or properly. There was no adult family member to speak for her and she could not speak for herself. Her roommate told us my mother fell out of the bed one night doing her short stay. I believe the cause of her death was more from improper care and lack of medication than anything else. She died in 1944 at the age of 27.

My father was stationed in a military base in or near New Orleans. Since no special consideration was given to black servicemen at that time, my father had to ride public transportation from New Orleans to Mobile. All blacks had to stand or be seated in the colored section of the bus. If there was no room, you would have to catch the next bus. It took my father three days to get to the hospital in Mobile and he did not get to see my mother before she passed, which made him angry and very bitter.

My Mother's Funeral

The sun was shining bright in the sky. It was one of those days when I would have been happily playing under the old oak tree in the back yard. Instead the family was gathered at the church where we all attended, waiting for the hearse to bring my mother from Mobile to Gosport. It did not seem real to me until the hearse arrived and the casket was brought into the church. I thought I would die on the spot. It was impossible to conceive that my beautiful mother was dead.

It was only three years after her mother passed. How could this be? MaMa and my mother both gone? Questions came into my head like a flood. "What will I do now? How can I live without my mother?" Fear of everything imaginable filled my head and unbelievable sorrow. This could not be happening. My whole world had fallen apart. I was ten years old and felt terribly alone.

My mother was the only child of Big Daddy and MaMa. The night before her funeral, Big Daddy spent most of the night building a wooden cross to put at the head of her grave. I had never seen him cry before that time. His demeanor exemplified a man who felt totally defeated. I wanted to reach out to him in some way and take the pain away, but my own grief was too overwhelming. My father suffered in silence and did not provide any comfort to me.

Soon after my mother passed, my father returned to the service and later received an honorable discharge from the army. He went to Mobile hoping to get his old job back but the department that he worked in had closed. His searches for employment lead him to move to Philadelphia, where his brothers lived. He was one of thousands of other blacks who were leaving the South, looking for employment and a better way of life.

My sister, brother and I did not want to move from our Big Daddy's house because it was our home where we were all born and spent every summer there when our parents were living in Mobile. Our cousins Ollie Lee, Jerri Lee and Otis lived with Big Daddy also. They were his sister's children and young adults. Otis was mentally challenged, and he would go away from the house and stay for a day or two sometimes and no one would know where he was. When he would return he would be dirty and looked as though he had been sleeping on the ground. I did not feel comfortable with Otis but cannot remember him ever causing a problem for anyone. He was obedient and did what he was told.

Big Daddy's House

I thought my grandfather was rich because we had one of the nicest houses in Gosport, a store and a car. The house and store were built by my grandfather on 13 acres of his land, which totaled 21 acres. The eight acres used for raising cotton were in another section not too far from the house, but far enough that we had to ride in the wagon to get there. The house had three bedrooms, a living room, dining room and kitchen and front and back porches. The front porch had a swing that we enjoyed tremendously.

There was a well in the back of our farmhouse with a Magnolia tree beside it. During the summer the smell of magnolia flowers filled the air. They were beautiful, and we would wear them in our hair like Billie Holiday wore her flower, on the side of her head. There was a productive fig tree on the side of the house, which served a dual purpose. Milk from the green figs was used on my skin when I had broken out with a rash. When the figs ripened, we ate them straight from the tree.

The smoke house, where meat was smoked and cured during hog killing time, was opposite the well and washing tubs were stationed on one side with a roof that extended over the tubs. They were conveniently located near the well, making it easy to draw water from the well and take it a short distance to the wash tubs. There was a big oak tree in the middle of the yard opposite the smoke house and our washing stations. A big black pot sat in the yard and we used it to boil the white clothes to get them white. A fire under the pot with flames shooting out on all sides was a remarkable sight. We had rub boards to help get the dirt out. We usually washed with homemade lye soap. We had clotheslines to hang the clothes and what could not fit on the lines went on the fences that surrounded the house.

The barn and barnyard were fenced in and sat on top of the hill adjacent to the house. Behind the smoke house was a large garden, peach trees, plum trees and pecan trees. Also, there was a state-of-the-art outhouse because there was no plumbing in the house. This outhouse had a cement floor that I thought was so neat. None of my friends had an outhouse with a cement floor. I never liked using it because it just felt so weird. The part that you sat on was made of wood with two round holes. Sometimes we had toilet paper but most times we used old newspaper or magazines.

We had a large barn that was fenced in and a fenced in area for the chickens. We had hogs, cows, and many chickens because my grandfather raised chickens and took them to Mobile to sell them. Our house was on a hill and the land went down the hill to the store. The pasture went out from the barn and down the hill. We had a large front yard that we kept swept clean with a straw broom. We planted flowers in the front and on the sides of the house.

Big Daddy's' store was an old-fashioned grocery store at the bottom of the hill, facing the highway. It was one large room with a small kitchen area for serving sandwiches. Steps in the front of the building lead you to the porch and front door. We sold fresh fish sandwiches, large pickles in a barrel, cheese, crackers, canned goods, bananas, ice cream, cakes, cookies, and candy galore. I ate so much ice cream and candy it was only by God's grace that I survived to become an adult.

Big Daddy had a relationship with a white man that brought him fresh fish every Saturday. We would clean and cook the fish before taking it to the store on Saturday evenings. Back then our deep fryer was the big four-legged pot that sat on the ground with fire underneath which served a dual purpose of bleaching the white clothes after scrubbing them on the washboard. It worked very well, and we could cook several fish at once.

Working in the store was our pleasure because it gave us the opportunity to socialize with many of the people in our community. It was quite different than at church. We could watch them dance to the music on the jukebox and have fun eating and drinking.

Monday through Friday was serious work time, whether it was chores after school or working in the field when school was not in session. The most time for pleasure was Saturday and Sunday after church. We took baths on Saturdays. We had a big tub that sat on the back porch and we took turns taking a bath. We heated water on the wooden stove for our bath and drew the cold water from the well. In my grandfather's house everyone went to church unless you were sick.

It was amazing how much work we accomplished in one Saturday. Getting up early, washing clothes, ironing, cooking cleaning house, washing and straightening our hair, taking our weekly bath and going to the store to work some more.

This was a wonderful place to grow up and live. We had a sense of security and wellbeing that was matchless. Fresh air, fresh food, and lots of work to do kept us busy. We were engaged in all the school and community activities, in addition to all the chores we had to do at home.

Everything was in walking distance except the land where my grandfather raised his crops, which were cotton, peanuts, and watermelons. Our main crop was Cotton. Big Daddy taught us at an early age how to work the cotton crop. After it was planted it had to be chopped and thinned out because it was altogether in bunches. Then as it got taller it had to be what we called hoed and cleared of weeds. Before long, it would bloom, and the cotton would come.

Cotton picking was a hard job and the hot sun beaming down on you did not help the situation. It was a backbreaker, and you had to start early in the morning and work all day except for the time you stopped to have lunch. We carried our lunch because it was too far to go home for lunch and come back. At the end of the day we were exhausted, so the ride on the wagon to get home was a pleasure. Dinner would be ready when we got home, and we would eat, wash our feet and go to bed.

This routine continued for a while. As is life, everything must change, and nothing remains the same. No matter how hard we worked on Saturday, on Sunday we went to church. Big Daddy was a Deacon in the church that we all attended and the only excuse for not going was sickness. My Big Daddy had rules that everyone had to follow.

While Big Daddy was dating and contemplating marriage our cousins, Ollie, Jerri and Otis, decided to move back to Mobile. Thinking back on the way we lived, it seems impossible that we could do so much in a day. The time seemed to be slower and the days seemed longer. Yet I say to myself, how can that be possible?

The first time I saw a movie was at my elementary school. Some white person brought a movie projector and screen to show movies at the school on Saturday nights. It was an exciting adventure to see people acting on the screen. I was so intrigued I wanted to be a movie star.

Occasionally my sister and I went to a real movie theater in Monroeville with some friends. We had to be seated in the colored section upstairs. The first time I was in a movie theater, "Gone with The Wind" was the main feature. I have always loved that movie and still look at it whenever I get the opportunity.

My sister and I went every place together. Big Daddy allowed my sister to date at the age of fifteen after much coercing by MaMa. I had to go with her on the few dates she had. I was not dating at the time being one year younger than she is. That did not stop the boys from talking to me. An opportunity to be with boys alone was against the rules. Big Daddy tried to protect us every way possible.

Other happy times were when Big Daddy gave me permission to stay overnight at my girlfriend's house or with another relative who lived in another town. Sometimes we went shopping for clothes in Grove Hill, Frisco City and Monroeville.

Early Childhood Thoughts

If I am a good girl and not do any harm to anyone then everyone will like me and want to be my friend. That was my mindset at the early age of five or six years old and continued into my teenage years when I began to see people differently. When I became a teen, I learned about envy and jealousy and how cruel people could be. I was very active in school, in Gosport, taking part in all the activities that were offered. I had the starring role in all the plays we presented at school, sang on the choir at school and at church, played basketball, softball and ran track also. I was very good at everything.

I was afraid of white people, which may have resulted from an incident when my sister and I had gone up the hill to the white man's store. As we were returning, two white boys started throwing rocks at us and calling us niggers. We tried to act brave, called them white soda crackers, and threw rocks back at them, but we hurried home and never told anyone about it. Maybe the other reason is we were never around white people except on very limited basics. We used to perform plays at my school and white people would come to see us perform. Other than seeing them in stores and on the streets whenever we went to the nearest town we had very little contact. Fear comes from not knowing. We fear anything that is unknown. Once we get to know the person, place or thing the fear is replaced with confidence.

CHAPTER TWO

Grandfather Takes a Bride

I do not know how long after my MaMa Carrie died that my Big Daddy met Lillie Bell Malone. She lived in Frisco City, Alabama. Her father's name was Joe Malone, a highly respected religious man, also a Deacon of his church. We called him Papa Joe. Papa Joe was a unique individual with the blackest skin I had ever seen and an outstanding singing ability that was different from anyone I knew. When we met him, he was married to his second wife, had nine children of his own, and was helping to raise his sister's children as well.

My sister, brother and I were very excited to meet such a large family. We felt like Bro. Rabbit being put in the briar patch. These beautiful people were: Lillie, Catherine, Mary, Marjorie, Amanda, John, Henry, Earnest, and Lewis. His sister's children were Wilma, Dan, Inez and Voncille. Papa Joe was a farmer with a lot of clout and a lot of land.

His house was a two-story; the only one that I knew existed in the black community. It was built about a half mile from the highway and you entered through a gate that led you on the road to the house. The house had a living room, kitchen, dining room and one bedroom on the first floor and on the second floor it had four bedrooms. There was a front porch also.

The landscaping was beautiful with large trees in the front and sides of the house and a large yard in the front and sides with beautiful flowers. The large barnyard was in the back and the land stretched for miles around. It was a beautiful sight when the crops were green in the fields and the flowers were blooming in the yard. It gave you a sense of security and peace that only comes from God.

My grandfather dated Lillie Bell, one of the oldest children, for what seemed to be a short time before they married. She moved into the house with us as we were living with him after my mother died and my father moved to Philadelphia. Lillie (Mama) was a beautiful woman, loving and kind. She treated us as though we were her own children. She had three children by Big Daddy, Barbara, John and Bud. Claudia and I helped to see after her children and we were like sisters and brothers, although they were our half Aunt and Uncles, our mother's half-sister and brothers.

The Denson and Malone Families

Life was great for us for a long time. We were happy spending time with the Malone Family because we were like brothers and sisters and there was always something going on. We worked hard in the fields, but we also had lots of fun playing games going to church and singing together. At one point we formed a singing group; the girls had a group and the boys had a group. We would go to different churches in and around the area and give concerts. It was so much fun. I had a high soprano voice and I was able to be the lead singer on some of the songs. We used to dress alike, and we always looked good.

We had the best food and the best cooks in the world. Everything was fresh because we grew all the food and raised all the meat that we ate, and it was plenty! The Malone's would come to our church in Gosport and we would go to theirs in Frisco City.

In our little country town, the school only went to the eight grades and you had to go someplace else. The two choices were Grove Hill or Perdue Hill. The most convenient for us was to go to Perdue Hill, which was close to where the Malones lived. My sister went to live with the Malones to finish High School. I was still in elementary school, which separated us for a while until I completed eighth grade and we both attended school together until she graduated high school.

My Big Change

I had a mean personality at an early age and I would scream and holler at people a lot. The grace of God saved me and changed my life. We attended Mackey Branch Baptist Church, which my Big Daddy helped to build, and his father was one of the founders of the same church. An annual tradition was established of having a revival service starting on the fourth Sunday in September. It would continue for a week with church services held every night Monday-Friday.

The beginning Sunday was called the Big Meeting. People who had moved from Gosport to live in cities like New York, Chicago, Philadelphia, Los Angeles, Detroit and many other places, would come home for this event. After the morning service, the grounds around the church would be set up like a giant picnic. Tables would be covered with all kinds of food and desserts. Lemonade was plentiful, and everyone had a joyous time eating and socializing.

I will never forget those times when we spent weeks preparing. The question of what to wear on this auspicious occasion was uppermost in our minds and sometimes we would order our dresses from the Montgomery Ward catalog. At one of these annual events something terrible happened. Everyone who attended these events did not come for the same reasons. People had their own agendas that were not always for the good of the community. Some would be in the woods behind the church doing all kinds of evil, like gambling, drinking moonshine and having affairs with women. I was very into everything and very inquisitive.

I was about the age of nine when this incident occurred. I should have been inside the church but instead I was outside in front of the church when I saw a man approach another man from behind. He was across the road in front of the church with an ax and he hit the other man in the head. It sounded very loud. The man fell down and his brains spilled out on the ground. It was a horrible gruesome sight to see. I will never forget that sight. My grandfather and other leaders in the community were quick to act and they subdued the assailant before he would get away. They held him in place until someone drove to the nearest town for the police, which was perhaps no more than fifteen miles away. The police came and arrested the man and took him to jail. That was the only bad incident I ever remember happening at our Revival meetings in Gosport.

It was during one of the revival times at the Mackey Branch Baptist Church that a great change came into my life. All the children who were not members of the church had to sit on the front seats called the mourners bench in front of the preacher. I sat there for two nights and listened to the preacher waiting for something to happen that I could not imagine. The third night, something spoke to my heart and said, "If you want to join the church you will have to get up and walk up to the preacher and give him your hand." I got up and walked up to the preacher and I felt like a burden had been lifted and I had been made new. Everyone who joined the church that week was baptized in the creek, down the road behind the church. I became a new person in Christ. My personality changed, and I became loving. I stopped hollering at people.

At the baptism I could not help but remember the time that Big Daddy had told my sister and I to stay away from the creek. We could not swim but liked to play in the water. One day some boys who were our friends came to our house and asked us to go to the creek with them. We disobeyed and went. We were playing in the water and having a great time when Big Daddy showed up with a long switch and beat us out of the water and all the way home.

A New Experience

Big Daddy was always the lead person in everything of good that happened in Gosport. Some white people decided to teach the black people in our community how to preserve food in jars, so they came to our house and all the women in the community came so they could learn. I guess the pressure cooker was a new instrument for cooking and canning foods, so they taught us how to do it. We had mason jars to put the food in and it was put into the jars and then into the pressure cooker. It was a great learning experience for us. We loved helping to get the food prepared and all the excitement of having so many people at our house. It was very helpful to have food already prepared that lasted all winter; we could open a jar and eat without so much work. We did not have much canned food because most of our food was planted and harvested from the garden or the fields.

During the time, we stayed at the Malone's house we had the experience of buying from the 'Rolling Store', which was a store on wheels. Someone thought of a way to make a large vehicle into a store with compartments to hold everything. It would be well stocked with canned goods, breads, cakes, candy, medicine and numerous other items. The owner of the rolling store had a regular routine and would start blowing his truck horn long before he arrived at the gate to Papa Joe's house, so we could meet him.

There were no stores in the area so this idea of bringing the store to the people was ingenious and really worked well for everyone. I was always happy to see the rolling store because

I could get candy and cookies like I was used to having on a regular basis at my grandfather's store.

A Grave Illness

At the age of eleven I developed diphtheria – a contagious disease in which a membrane formed in my throat and made it very difficult for me to swallow. It could have caused choking or death. In my case I developed a very high fever and had to be isolated from the rest of the family. We went to a white doctor named Dr. Browden, in Claiborne. Big Daddy took me in his car for one week straight. It was about half an hour from where we lived. Dr. Browden injected medication into my arm and mopped my throat with medicine each time. He was a kind old man and gave specific instructions on how to take care of me.

The doctor told Big Daddy to bury all my body waste and keep me isolated from the rest of the family. From time to time my fever was so high I would see dead people. I thought my mother and grandmother were in white garments looking like angels and walking around my bed. I screamed and was very afraid because I believed they were real. Mama took excellent care of me and the rest of the family. It must have been very difficult for her because she had three small children to take care of as well. She never complained and loved and treated is as if we were her own.

After the encounter with the angels I was healed, and life became normal again. Because of the excellent care I received from Mama, and the Grace of God, I was saved.

New Discoveries

During my elementary school days, the 4-H Club was introduced to our community. It was a good organization that helped young people to develop new skills, explore possible career choices, and serve their communities. The four H's stand for head, heart, hands, and health. Members showed their high ideals with their motto 'To Make the Best Better', and with their pledge: "I pledge My head to clearer thinking, My heart to greater loyalty, My hands to larger service, and My health to better living, for my club, my community, my country, and my world."

My grandfather had connections, which gave my sister Claudia, and I an opportunity to go to a 4-H camp in the summer in Grove Hill for two weeks. We met other black children from other communities in Alabama. We had lots of fun, made new friends and learned a lot.

It was a time when we were getting older and becoming interested in boys. I also experienced my period and didn't have a clue as to why I was bleeding. I was eleven years old and had heard the older girls talk about girls who came to school without taking a bath. At a certain time of the month you were not supposed to take a bath. I do not know where that came from. Nevertheless, I used to get away from those girls who did not take a bath during that certain time of the month because they smelled horrible. I felt wetness in my panties and I knew I was not peeing on myself, so I went into the closet to investigate.

When I saw the blood, I was petrified and thought I was bleeding to death. I kept wiping myself to try to wipe it away, but it kept coming. I ran in and out of the closest so many times my sister noticed and asked me, "What is wrong with you?" "I don't know – I am bleeding," was my reply as I trembled with fear. She assured me that I was okay. She had experienced her period long before me and she was so kind and understanding. We did not have sanitary napkins from the store, so we had to make a pad from old clean material, like sheets or old clothing, that we cut into pieces to fit comfortably inside our panties. At some point, we were able to buy Kotex from the store. It brings tears to my eyes now when I think about how close my sister and I have always been. She has always protected me whenever she could and taught me many things. I was not always a good child. I had a mean personality at an early age and I would scream and holler at people a lot including my sister.

For six years after my mother passed my life took many twists and turns. My body changed, and I changed from a hollering brat to an inquisitive young woman. Big Daddy was overly protective and did not want my sister and me to date boys. He was so afraid that we would become pregnant before we received our education. Many girls in the community were getting pregnant and he would always say so and so got 'big'. Big Daddy never explained how you get 'big'. What he said was, "Keep your dress tail down and stay away from boys." I developed such a complex; I thought that if I kissed a boy I would become 'big'. Finishing high school and college was what was expected, and Big Daddy would not accept anything less.

Big Daddy would have given his life for his family, but lack of education limited him in many ways that would have benefited us. We did not have a clue as to what he meant by the statement of keeping our dress tail down. All we needed was a simple explanation about sex and how children are conceived. Not being taught about sex left me vulnerable and unprepared to teach my own children.

What I Wish I Had Been Taught

Your body is special and wonderfully made by God to be able to reproduce. When you become about ten or eleven you will have a menstrual cycle, which is a few days of bleeding from your vagina. It is a natural necessary function that allows you to become a mother. Where is the vagina? It is that part of the body below your stomach between your legs. It will grow hair at the appropriate time. You may experience warm feelings when you touch the area and if you put your finger inside. These feelings are normal, and some people will take it a step further to get more pleasure which is called masturbation. I would not recommend this behavior because it could become a habit.

You have inside the middle of your body a pear-shaped organ; a uterus (womb) where the baby will grow. Something miraculous happens every month in the ovaries located on either side of the uterus: an egg a month is released, capable of developing into a baby. After it matures inside the ovary it travels through the fallopian tube located on either side of the uterus to the inside of the uterus and attaches to the wall of the uterus where food stored in the blood has made a lining for the egg to live and grow if it is fertilized by a male sperm.

If fertilization occurs (egg and sperm joining together), it takes place in the fallopian tube. How does the male sperm get to the egg? If you have sex with a male and he releases his sperm from his penis (dick) into your vagina and it connects with the egg as it is traveling through the fallopian tube, a baby is formed. Normally the baby will grow inside of the womb for nine months before it comes out through the vagina. The vagina is where the baby comes out from the uterus. If a month goes by and the egg is not fertilized, the blood lining is not needed. The egg and blood will be discharged through the vagina – hence your period.

This first-time sexual experience is so important that God said in the Bible it should be between a man and a woman who are married. The emotional fall out is so great that it leaves an indelible impression on your mind that you will never forget. Females are very emotional and nurturing human beings. If you make a mistake and give yourself to the wrong person, it leaves a very bad feeling that is hard to recover from. Females give themselves in the name of love, whereas the male may only be interested in a conquest, so he can brag to his friends.

In some cultures, a female is tested on their wedding night to confirm that they are virgins (meaning they have never had sex before marriage). If a woman has never had sex the membrane that covers the opening of the womb is usually still intact until the male penis pushes into it causing it to break and some bleeding will occur. If there is no bleeding now, the female may not be able to prove that she is a virgin. This bleeding happens once and is not connected with a regular monthly period. You will not have a menstrual cycle during normal pregnancy although sometimes it happens and causes a miscarriage and you lose the baby.

The menstrual cycle is nothing to be afraid of even though it may cause some discomfort in the form of headaches, bloating, cramping and irritability from time to time. It is up to you to choose to take care of your body and treat it with respect. You only get one, so be conscious of your decisions and the consequences. Think for yourself, and trust God to make wise decisions.

Proverbs 2:6-7 (KJV) For the Lord giveth wisdom: out of his mouth cometh knowledge and understanding. "He layeth up sound wisdom for the righteous: he is a buckler to them that walk uprightly.

The amount of blood discharged during menstruation varies with the individual. Sometimes a period will last 2-3 or 2-5 days, but the blood loss is not enough to cause a girl to become anemic or weaken her. The body quickly replaces this small amount of blood. Your period may be irregular for the first couple of years, and you may miss two or three months between periods. After that, the cycle should recur every 26 to 30 days. Excitement or nervousness may cause irregularity. Many girls skip menstrual periods when a great change in their normal routine occurs; for example, when they are away at summer camp or during their first year at college. If you are not sexually active and miss your period, you have nothing to worry about. On the other hand, if you are, be very worried if you are not ready to have a baby.

Not having sex before marriage with a male who hasn't had sex is for your own protection: Neither of you can bring a disease that comes from having sex with a person who has a sexually transmitted infection (STI) or sexually transmitted disease (STD) or Venereal disease (VD). These diseases are commonly spread by having sex, especially vaginal intercourse, anal sex and oral sex. Vaginal sex is when the penis goes inside the vagina. Anal sex is when the penis goes into the rectum. Oral sex is when the penis is put inside of the mouth.

During your teenage and young adult years, concentrate on you and spend your time learning all you can about life, your personal preferences, your family and everything that will make you a well-rounded individual. Spend time discovering the gifts that God gave you. We all have gifts and sometimes it takes a while to know what they are. You have so much to learn and the quicker you learn the better. Take advantage of every opportunity to learn music, art, cooking, sports, exercises like skating and swimming, learn challenging games like chess and golf. Abstain from sex and bad behavior e.g. smoking any substance, taking drugs, illegal or legal, drinking alcohol, or mistreating your body in any way. Be a responsible person, obedient to your parents, and respectful of the law and follow the rules of our society. Being wild and acting crazy will only get you in trouble and cause much heartache for you and your family.

You are in control of your body and let no one take advantage of you. If a male assaults you and rapes you, call the police and report it right away. Don't hold it inside of you, because it will cause you much pain.

Bizarre Stuff at School

In Gosport I was very popular in school, participating in almost every activity the school offered. The boys all seemed to like me, and I wanted the attention. I decided to cause a problem for a girl that I did not like by writing to her boyfriend. So, I wrote to him and asked him to meet me at the women's outhouse. I cannot imagine what I was thinking. It was a stupid gesture.

My teacher was very shrewd and noticed that I was writing in my composition book and not paying attention to what was going on in the class. During recess she looked in my book and read my letter. At the end of the day, my teacher stopped at Big Daddy's house and told Mama what I had done. Mama told my Big Daddy when he came home, and I received one of the worst beatings of my life. He made me lie across the bed and he beat me with a strap. My behind was sore for a week. I did not write any more tales to anyone after that. It was a lie from the beginning. I did not intend to meet that boy anywhere. I was trying to get some attention away from the other girl.

My parents taught me to respect my elders and those who were in authority. One of my ninth-grade teachers at the high school I attended in Perdue Hill did something very strange as I sat in a classroom with four or five other students.

The chairs were arranged in a semicircle and his chair was next to mine. He was close enough to me to be able to rub my arm and I could not tell if the other students could see what he was doing. I was very uncomfortable but did not want to bring attention to what he was doing in case they were not aware.

When class was over, he announced that we were going on an excursion, which was simply a walk across the yard to the woods nearby. All the students in the class left early except for one boy named Skip and me. Skip said he had to go someplace and he would meet us later. The teacher and I proceeded to walk into the woods alone. I was nervous and afraid but felt that I had to obey the teacher. We walked what seemed like a short distance but far enough to not be seen from the school windows facing the woods.

I do not remember what he actually said about anything (he was supposed to be teaching me about the trees or flowers), but I do remember him gently grabbing me by the arm and pulling me close to him and kissing me on the lips, at which time I panicked. I was afraid Skip would come any minute and see what was happening. I felt a deep sense of guilt and shame because I felt that this man had allowed himself to lose control and I thought it was my fault. He was a married man who happened to be living with his pregnant wife in Papa Joe's house where I was also staying, and I was going to the school where he was teaching.

After the kiss, I pulled away and started walking fast to get out of the woods. He just followed me without saying anything. By the time we were coming out of the woods, Skip was coming toward us. He was a little too late to save us from a scandal. When I got back to the classroom, I was summoned immediately to the Principal's office. The teacher in the adjacent classroom had seen us going into the woods and reported to the Principal. I knew I was in trouble but did not feel that I had done anything wrong.

The Principal was a very strict older gentleman who was well educated and respected in the community. His questions were relentless. I knew that the teacher kissing me was wrong, but I did not want to cause harm to my teacher's wife or cause him to lose his job. Therefore, I lied at first and told the Principal that nothing happened.

The questions kept coming, "Why did you go into the woods? What did he do to you? Why were you coming out as Skip was going in?" I tried to protect us both, but the tears started to flow, and I became very emotional. The Principal said, "If you were a willing participant in whatever happened then you are as much at fault as the teacher."

I was not attracted to this man nor was I pursuing him; he was a grown man and I was a fifteen-year-old. I wanted to clear myself, so I told him the truth. I said, "He kissed me and that was all that happened." The teacher was called into the office and must have been fired immediately. The wheels of justice turned very swiftly and the same week it happened he packed up his wife and left town. Neither he nor his wife ever said anything to me and the next thing I knew they were gone.

I felt so much guilt after that incident. I never told anyone about it until school was out and I was at home again. One day Mama Lillie Bell and I were relaxing in my room and talking about school and other things. I believe she asked me what happened, and I told her the whole story. It was a big scandal around the school and people were talking about it in the community. I felt very bad and wondered what happened to the teacher and his wife long after the incident, but never heard from them again.

Lucky for me it was my last year at that school and I did not have to be there the next year and be humiliated and talked about. The next year my sister and I moved to Philadelphia to live with our father, stepmother and brother. I began a whole new chapter in my life and met the man I would marry.

Good Times Before the Storm

During this extraordinary time when things were good, Mama attended College in Selma, Alabama at the University. Her brother Lewis (called LC) had returned from the armed forces and was living with us. He attended college at Tennessee State. I do not know why Mama's brother came to live with us, which proved to be detrimental to me. Perhaps Big Daddy needed help at that time. Our cousins, Ollie, Jerri, and Otis had moved on with their lives and were living in Mobile.

And as life happens, Big Daddy became ill suddenly and had to have an appendectomy. His boss, Mr. Bush, was instrumental in helping him to get to the hospital quickly, which saved his life. Big Daddy had a slow recovery and never seemed to get back to normal after that incident.

When Big Daddy became ill again he would not recover. He had a talk with LC and asked him to take care of the family. We would all visit him in the hospital and were with him when he took his last breath. I will never forget that moment. It was as if my world had suddenly ended. I was afraid for the first time in my young adult life. What would we do? I did not want to leave the South to live with my father who had remarried and was living in Philadelphia. Philadelphia was like some zillion miles away and I did not want to go there.

My life changed drastically. Mama was as good as always and treated us the same, but circumstances changed, and she needed help financially to take care of her children and us.

My father had a low-income job and did not send enough money often enough. My brother was getting out of hand and being disrespectful. Therefore, he was the first to have to go and live with our father. Claudia and I managed to hold out a little longer by working hard and being obedient. In hindsight, it would have been better if we had left when our brother left.

My sister Claudia was in 12th grade and had to live with Papa Joe to finish high school. By this time, I was in the 9th grade and had to live with Papa Joe to attend school. At one point we were separated; she was at Papa Joe's and I was at home with Mama and LC. Mama was teaching school in the next little town called Little Rock and she took her three children to school where she worked. I was attending the elementary school just up the hill from our house. I walked to school every day.

One day something awful happened. This day I was playing in the yard and home alone. School had not started but Claudia was not home, and neither was Mama or the children. I do not remember why I was home alone with LC. I did not have a problem playing by myself under the big oak tree in the backyard of the house. LC approached me and asked me, "Do you want to get a new pair of shoes for school?" School would be starting soon and of course I wanted a new pair of shoes. I thought to myself, "Don't I always get a new pair of shoes for school?" I said, "yes" without any hesitation. He said, "If you want a new pair of shoes you will have to meet me in the bedroom and do what I say." I was more interested in the new shoes than what was about to happen to me. My knowledge about sex was limited to hearing Big Daddy talk about who was made big. It was not taught in our elementary school either. I was fifteen years old and ignorant and naïve as to what this grown man was about to do.

I buried this secret for most of my adult life. When I decided to write about my life it surfaced, and I had to deal with it. I have been struggling with forgiveness for some time and this is one of the main pieces. The guilt has been nagging at me and I feel so ashamed. I have prayed and asked God to forgive me and enable me to forgive LC.

I consented to do what he said for a pair of new shoes. I went in the house and met him in the bedroom. He said, "Lie across the bed." He took off my panties, put on a condom, which we called a rubber, and straddled me and began to try to push his penis inside of my vagina. It was very painful and would not fit at all, but God was merciful and in LC's excitement he did not last long, and I was spared from penetration. Later, I read a book about intercourse and how it happens in the head and does not last but several minutes. Thank God he did not last but a few minutes.

This was my introduction to sex and I did not want any part of it. The questions came to my mind, such as, "Is this what I have to look forward to? Why would anybody want to do that?" I knew I had sinned and felt very ashamed. I would never tell anyone, and I kept it hidden until I decided to write about my life. This incident was a prelude to what would come before my sister and I moved to Philadelphia.

I knew I had been taken advantage of when Mama came home from school and announced to me that she would be taking me to Claiborne the next day to get a new pair of shoes. I wanted to disappear at that moment but would have killed LC before if it had been possible.

CHAPTER THREE

Moving from Gosport to Philadelphia

While the idea of moving to a new city was exciting, it was also scary. I was sixteen and very naïve about everything. Many questions were floating around in my head. I wondered where I would go to school, what grade they would put me in, and how I would get along with the white children in the school. Because I did not like white people it was hard to imagine me enjoying being in a classroom with them. I did not discuss these fears with anyone. I tried to be brave and kept it all inside.

On the long drive from Gosport to Philadelphia, in my father's car, I had plenty of time to ponder on everything that crowded my mind. While riding through Washington, DC we were shocked to see houses attached to one another. That was certainly not the norm for us and I could not understand why people would live like that. No separation, no yard and no grass, how horrible! We thought the whole city was attached. Our disappointment came early before we arrived in Philadelphia. Of course, we did not see the upscale section of the city where the fabulous single homes were.

It was a relief to arrive safely in the 1400 block of Ogden Street in North Philadelphia where my father, stepmother, her sister and niece lived. It was a modest three-story house. My sister and I shared a room on the second floor. When we arrived, my brother was no longer living with my father as he had gotten into some gang trouble and was in a special school for boys.

Our relationship with our brother was never the same after he left Gosport. He chose a different path. Growing up we shared everything. Once we had a bicycle that the three of us had to take turns riding. My parents treated us fairly and we had the same rules to follow, but my brother decided to make his own rules and he suffered the consequences of his bad decisions.

A New Beginning

Change can be difficult because we fear the unknown. A new environment, new rules to follow, new personalities to learn to deal with, a big city to learn and all-around change was challenging. I was raised by my grandfather to be obedient to my parents and elders, so I did not have a problem with that. Having to be enrolled into a new school meeting new people was a little scary. I really did not know my father very well because of his time away in the service, and the separation after my mother passed and he moved to Philadelphia. I didn't know my stepmother Julia at all, only having met her once when my father came to get my brother. She looked like my mother, with light skin and freckles on her face. Her personality was quite different.

We all did our best to adjust and get along. Her sister Martha and her niece were living with them at the time. Our cousin, Birdie (my father's niece), came with us and stayed for several months before returning to Mobile. We called Julia "Mother" from our first meeting. Mother was kind and made it easy for me to feel better about school by introducing me to Delores, who was the daughter of Rev. Thomas. They lived around the corner on 15th Street, across from Second Pilgrim Baptist Church where he was the Pastor.

Delores was attending William Penn High School for Girls, where I had to attend. It was located at 15th and Wallace Streets, before relocating to Broad Street. Delores and I became instant friends and went to school together. I was happy to know someone who would be in the same school.

Mother took me to the school to be enrolled and tested and to be placed in the proper grade. I passed the test and was put into the 10th grade.

In high school in Philadelphia I continued to be active, playing basketball, singing in the school choir, and acting in one school play, as a maid. I did not qualify for the lead role as in Gosport. Before graduation, we were given a group of aptitude tests that all the students had to take before graduation. Our evaluation was on many levels of aptitude and the results were given individually. The person that gave me my results was a white man and it appears he got a lot of pleasure in telling me that I did good on everything but was not outstanding in anything.

The way he said it hurt me very deeply because I thought he was a redneck that got pleasure in degrading black people. Of course, it made me cry, because I cried at everything that made me feel bad. I was deeply emotional and sensitive to whatever was going on that was not good, even when I was not the person involved. I wanted so badly to see the good in everyone until it was difficult for me to know when someone was trying to take advantage of me. I did not learn that lesson until much later in life, after I was married and had several children. My husband taught me all about not trusting people and how cruel people could be, including him.

Cupid's Arrow

One day my sister Claudia and my cousin Birdie and I were standing outside of our house in the 1400 block of Ogden Street, talking and playing around when this fine young, tall, dark and handsome man walked out of his house from across the street and went around the corner. All our eyes were on him and he knew it. I doubt if he had to go any place because he had already checked us out from his living room window before he left his house. I felt cupid's arrow shoot straight through my heart when I saw him for that first time, and I knew I wanted to marry him.

His name was Charles Bronner. We were born in the same year, 1934; my birth date was May 11th and his June 26th. We came from similar small country towns. He was born in Kelly, Georgia. His father came from a family of eleven children and his father's parents were bigtime landowners in Kelly. His parents married at an early age and had three children, two girls and a boy. Charles' mom and dad lived with his parents after marriage until they decided to move to Pennsylvania, first to Pottstown, where his mother's sister Elvira lived, and then to Philadelphia. We were brought up in loving homes, with strong religious roots.

Two guys from our hometown, Dan and Henry, relatives of our step grandmother (Mamma), had moved to Philadelphia previously and they knew Charles. Dan was dating my sister and Henry was dating my cousin. I was the only one available and not dating anyone. Charles and I were destined to be together. Charles asked Dan to introduce me to him and we were first introduced over the telephone. Later Charles came over to my house and wanted to take me out that night, but my parents would not agree for me to go out with him. I think it was because it was a little late to be going out. He was very aggressive and did not have a problem asking for what he wanted.

After that first meeting at my house we were inseparable. We did everything we could do together, and I was true to our relationship because I loved him unconditionally. I know he loved me very much, but his love was mixed with possessiveness. One night some male friends from our hometown came by to visit us, and Charles was looking out the window of his house and saw them. It was a little late and my sister and I had our pajamas on, but we let them come in. In a few minutes, after they were inside, Charles came over and demanded that I go upstairs. He had been looking out of his window as usual to see who was coming and going out of our house. I went upstairs because I did not want to have any trouble out of him, but my sister was furious with us both.

His feelings for me did not stop him from looking and getting fresh with other women every chance he got. He had a way with people and could get his way in most cases. We were both in high school in different areas of the city. His school, Frankford High, was co-ed and had an almost all white enrollment in the Northeast section of the city. My school, William Penn, was the exact opposite, all girls, with an almost all black enrollment in North Philadelphia. Because of his own insecurities and extreme jealousy, Charles loved the fact that I went to an all-girls school because he did not have to worry about me meeting other boys. We both graduated high school the same year and attended each other's proms.

This man knew how to do many things. He was unafraid to speak for himself and could convince others to agree with him on many ideas that were unconventional. I, on the other hand, was afraid to speak up and tell my true feelings. He taught me how to talk to people about business, how to drive a car, and how not to trust everyone. I was 16 years old and so naïve when we first met. He was the same age but twice my age in knowledge about the world and people. I fell in love at first sight and he was very overprotective and jealous. He did not want anyone to look at me and demanded that I dress in a manner that would not bring attention, like cleavage showing, nothing too short or too tight, no shorts allowed. Make-up was limited to face powder and lipstick. I was crazy in love with him and allowed him to dictate my life.

After I graduated from high school I was becoming bored with our relationship as it was. He was very sexual and taught me that sex was very different and enjoyable between a man and a woman in love. While I enjoyed the encounters, it made me feel guilty, as I believed what the Bible says about sex, that it should be between a man and woman who are married. He wanted to have sex to a degree that made it seem he was addicted to it. I was not going to be dictated to without the benefit of marriage. After five years I told him I wanted to move on.

He was my only boyfriend from the first time we met at sixteen. I loved him unconditionally and felt that five years was enough time without benefit of marriage. He decided to buy an engagement ring and asked me to marry him. Our wedding was scheduled for September 1955, but as fate would have it I discovered I was pregnant with my oldest daughter. We cancelled the wedding plans and went to his parents' preacher's house and were married with his younger sister, Hazel, as the only witness on August 6, 1955.

We flew to New York for a honeymoon weekend. It was our first flight on an airplane and we were excited and very happy to be married. I was not so happy to be pregnant at that time. I wanted to have children, but I also wanted to have a conventional wedding with all my family there. Therefore, it caused me to have mixed emotions. At that time, I also had a decent job with the government. I had spent a lot of time after high school on menial jobs because of not being qualified to get a decent job. I had taken college courses in high school thinking I was going to college. Had I received proper counseling in school I would have been prepared to get a decent job when I finished.

When I talked to my counselor, I made it clear that I wanted to go to college, but did not know how I would get financing to go. My parents did not have money and there were no student loans at that time. I did not take typing until my senior year and I could not type when I graduated high school. After graduating and realizing I had to get a job and go to college or business school to prepare for any well-paying job, I enrolled in Temple University's Business Administration night school program, on Spring Garden Street, and I worked during the day.

My first job was called Busboy at a cafeteria in center city Philadelphia, on Market Street. It was a place where people could get their food buffet style find a table and sit and eat. My job was to clear the dishes and wash the tables. It was a thriving business and very busy especially at lunchtime. It was backbreaking work and you never had time to sit down. I lasted 3 weeks and I quit.

The next job I did was filling in for my cousin Catherine Cromartie. She was a waitress in Jimmy's; a very busy restaurant located on Ridge Avenue. She was also pursuing a modeling career. Catherine was sick and needed someone to replace her for three days. That was about as much as I could take at that job. The boss was very hard to deal with. He wanted you to be able to tell how much the customer owed from the food that they had eaten. I was happy when Catherine returned to work.

My next job was at a coat factory. There were plenty of jobs in the 1950's and 60's in Philadelphia. Factories of every kind were all over the city and Help Wanted signs were everywhere. I was in the coat factory, but the coat factory was not in me. I was taking college courses at night and working at the factory doing the day. As soon as I developed my typing skills, I took the government test for Clerk-Typist and passed. I got the job and began working at the Custom House at 2nd and Chestnut Streets. I was a happy camper!

My experience at the coat factory was daunting. The employees were mainly Italians who showed little respect for their bosses or anyone else. Every day was filled with loud cussing and swearing. I was not accustomed to either, so I felt very out of place and intimidated every day. My job was to match the collar to the coat when it came to my station. The system was to match by number sometimes the numbers were not right. I would get hollered at when the collar did not match the coat. I was timid and afraid when the cussing would start and be directed at me. It was terrible. I felt so out of place surrounded by Italians who spoke mostly Italian and I didn't speak their language. There were a few black people employed there but none of them worked in my area. I would gravitate to their area and have a peaceful lunch each day.

Lunchtime and quitting time were the best times of the day for me. When God answered my prayer and allowed me to get a decent job, I was the happiest person and so grateful for God's mercy and grace. I told everyone there that I was leaving for a better job. Most of the people were happy for me especially my black friends. I was doing fine in my new job as a clerk typist with the Civil Service Commission in downtown Philadelphia. My position was a step up from what I was doing previously. After I started working for the government I helped my husband apply for and get a job with another government agency. The first was the Signal Corps. We were both good at our jobs and getting along well.

My attitude about white people started to change as I matured and made friends with a few co-workers who were white. I never tried to be friends with any of my white classmates in high school. The fear about white people was related to what I knew about slavery. I thought that all white people were evil. Knowledge is powerful, but fear comes from the not knowing. My mindset began to change as I realized that God created all people, and we all aspire to be loved and respected by other human beings. When you know better you do better. The knowledge I gained from association with white people made me know that the major difference is only skin color. All races of people have similar problems, desires and aspirations.

A Cruel Test

My husband was a quick thinker, never lost for words or afraid to express his opinion. He loved to debate with people on worldly issues and whatever the current events were at any given time. He was also a good liar and sometimes could convince people that he was telling the truth. One day he decided to put me through a test and his mother was involved. He called and asked me to come over to his mom's house; nothing unusual about that but when I arrived he and his mom were sitting in the living room waiting for me. I had a suspicious feeling as though it was a set-up, but I wanted to know the reason, so I went along. He greeted me politely offered me a seat and started his story.

He said, "I talked to your doctor today and asked him, why you have stretch marks on your body? The doctor said it could have come from you being pregnant." I responded, "What? I have never been pregnant, and if I was I am sure I would know it." Looking for support from his mother, I asked her, "If I had ever been pregnant I would know it wouldn't I?" Her answer was "yes", without hesitation. I became so emotional and upset that I was crying.

He went on to say that he was breaking up with me because he thought that I had a child before I came to Philadelphia. He went further and said that someone told him I had a child down south. I felt like I was on trial and had just been sentenced to death. My heart was pounding, and tears were uncontrollable. I asked him, "Who told you that lie? It is not true, and I want to know that person's name, so I can defend myself." He did not respond but commenced to gather framed pictures of us that were always in the living room of his parent's home and handed them to me. I felt as though I was being thrown out like a piece of trash, but I gathered up as much self-respect as I could muster and started out the door with pictures in hand.

I only had to go across the street to my house, and luckily no one was home to question me about the pictures I was carrying. I went straight to my room, closed the door and tried to shut out the world. I could not tell anyone, so I cried and prayed to God for an answer to this horrific dilemma. What do I do now? I was so distraught and angry I wanted to kill him.

I allowed my love for him to overshadow everything I did. Whatever he wanted was what I went along with, even when I didn't agree with it. I had such a love for him that when things didn't go well with us I felt severely depressed. I would have given my life for this man.

That kind of love is unacceptable in my opinion today, and I feel it was way over the top for me or anyone else. I am overflowing with joy in my heart that God has allowed me to live long enough to look back and see the mistakes I made. Hopefully I can help someone else to not make the same mistakes by sharing my life and experiences. I believe in love and marriage between a man and a woman, but I don't believe in one person taking advantage of another. I believe in mutual respect.

Later that same evening I received a phone call from Charles concerning the pregnancy issue. He apologized for the things he said and assured me that he still wanted to marry me. My reaction was proof enough for him that I was being truthful.

I still wanted to marry him in addition to punishing him. To get revenge, I would treat him cruelly for a period, until I felt better and forgave him.

A Great Opportunity!

I was feeling very secure in my life when Nathaniel Hawthorne Bronner Sr., Founder of the Bronner Brothers Hair Care Company of Atlanta, came to visit and offered my husband a job in Atlanta. Charles' father, Charlie Bronner, was Nathaniel's uncle, which made my husband his first cousin. Nathaniel was very fond of his uncle Charlie and visited whenever possible.

Shortly after we were married Nathaniel offered my husband a supervisory position with the BB Company and the opportunity to invest in the company. It was a once in a lifetime offer that Charles said he would think about. Charles and I had saved a couple thousand dollars (a lot of money in the 50's) to buy a house before we were married, and not having made the investment we were living with his parents. I was not happy living across the street from my parents after we were married. It was like I had not made any progress, just moved across the street.

I was thrilled about this opportunity and Charles seemed excited also. I was not too happy about leaving my job, but knowing that I would have to leave before my baby was born made it easier to accept. Charles moved to Atlanta first and I came down two weeks later. I wanted to give my job two weeks' notice and give myself time to prepare. I was pregnant at the time and had to buy some new clothes, as my regular clothes were not comfortable anymore. It was the best and worst of times for me because I had not gotten used to being married, pregnant, and having to adjust to a new city and not being with my family was onerous. I felt completely comfortable with Charles' family in Atlanta, but not so much with him.

When I moved to Atlanta, I found my husband to be a very different person. He was living in a large house with Emma Bronner-Lewis and her husband Henderson Lewis. Emma was the sister of Nathaniel Bronner Sr. and we affectionately called her "Polly". Polly and her husband were a very loving couple and they were respectful of each other. It was a joy to see them together. Polly was a beautician and operated her own beauty shop. Nathaniel used to sell beauty products from his home and his sister's shop before he opened his first business on Auburn Avenue. I felt very comfortable in their home and Polly and her husband helped me to learn to cook and shop for groceries. My husband, on the other hand, found time for everybody except me. He spent more of his non-working hours in the street than at home.

Shortly after I arrived he informed me that he was going to buy a car. I asked the question, "What about investing in the company?" His reply was, "I am not going to invest in the company." I could not believe my ears and was disappointed that this man was so selfish that he would decide on his own without asking my opinion. Both of us saved the money we had, and I felt I should have a say in what we did with it. Rather than having an argument, I agreed to let him have his way. One day soon after, he came home with a new Oldsmobile that took the place of a great opportunity. From that day forward, I did not know what the car cost or how much money we had left or if we had any money left. I decided to be the homemaker and mother and let him worry about taking care of our baby and me.

He blew the opportunity to invest in the company and that opportunity has never been offered again. Having transportation gave him more freedom to go and do whatever he wanted to do. I believe that he loved me, but I do not believe he was ready to make a commitment to one woman. As time went on, and he was home with me less and less, I became suspicious that he was having an affair. A woman who knows her man can always tell if he is having an affair because of the changes that occur with him and his attitude. I do not think a man can cheat without some change in his behavior. I could always tell when it was happening and when it would stop for a period and a new one would start.

It was a pleasure to meet Nathaniel's wife Robbie, and we became instant friends. We had a lot in common, not the least of which was both of us being pregnant with our first child. We had the same doctor and delivered our babies at the same hospital, two weeks apart. The name of the hospital was Hughes Spaulding. Robbie and I spent some quality time together and were supportive of each other. I learned a lot and grew spiritually from attending her Bible classes. It is interesting how our lives ran parallel. Our first babies were born two weeks apart, hers being a boy and mine a girl, and it continued as the years progressed. Each time she had a boy, I had a girl and I ended up with six girls and she had six boys.

Nathaniel's younger sister, Juanita Bronner- Garmon, was a major part of the BB Company and helped to make it what it is today. Also, Nathaniel's brother, Arthur E. Bronner (whom we affectionately called Mr. A.E.), was a major investor and Nathaniel's right-hand man. Juanita was my husband's favorite cousin and although they worked together he could not come straight home from work without stopping at Juanita's house.

Charles and I went to church and many social affairs with Juanita and her husband, Roscoe Garmon. We were good friends and spent some awe-inspiring times together in their home, cooking eating and playing games. Juanita was like a sister to both of us and we loved her dearly. She was a sweet person with a big heart who loved people. Her loving husband was a hardworking, independent family man and a good provider.

Having My First Baby

Being pregnant was scary, strange and different. Being away from home made it scarier. I had the biggest appetite and would eat large boxes of Kellogg's Corn Flakes. I followed the doctor's orders, exercised, and took my vitamins. I spent a lot of time learning to cook using my encyclopedia cookbook. When I felt the baby kick for the first time, I was astonished and did not know what it was. A question came to mind, "What is that? Is this the baby kicking?" It was not long before I realized there was a lot more to come. I was home alone when it happened the first time and felt surprised and concerned. I did not tell anyone and decided to wait and figure it out on my own. It did finally register in my brain that it had to be the baby kicking.

My stomach got really big and it became difficult to get up from a sitting position. The baby kicking was annoying and interfered with my sleeping. My water broke on February 1, 1956 and my daughter was not born until February 2. I was in labor for an entire 24 hours. I thought I was going to die before my baby came. It was such a relief when she was born.

I had been cut from front to back and I could not sit down without pain for about two weeks. My baby was 8 lbs. with a head full of black hair and as pretty she could be. We named her Deborah Rene Bronner. We called her Debbie. Her grandmother Obie (Charles' Mother) came to Atlanta and stayed with us for a few days after Debbie was born.

Wherever we took Debbie people would stop us to say how pretty she was. I thanked God for giving me a healthy baby and it was okay that she was also pretty.

It was a little hard not having family there and no one to babysit. I felt isolated and sometimes lonely when Charles was in the street. My time was spent taking care of the baby and learning to cook. Some days I would walk the baby to the parks, which were a few blocks from the house, and on one occasion Robbie came to visit me with Nathaniel Jr. who was two weeks older than my Deborah. We enjoyed walking in the park and sharing experiences of being new mothers.

One night my husband went out and left Deborah and I home. I was very upset and tried to get someone to keep the baby, so I could look for him. I could not get anyone, so I decided to be dressed when he returned home and be ready to leave when he came in. I did exactly that but when I walked out the door, he walked out behind me and left the baby alone. I was only bluffing but he called my bluff because he knew I would never leave my baby home alone. I walked about a block up the street and turned around and came home. I was not going to leave my baby home alone for anybody.

He turned out to be extremely jealous and insecure. I thought if I did not give him any reason to be jealous he would trust me. I was never flirtatious or interested in another man. I loved my husband and did not want another man, but I was unable to convince him that not all women cheat. This thing he had about women cheating was deeply rooted in him and it didn't matter what I said or did, he would accuse me from time to time.

Beware of a person who is accusing you of doing wrong; their guilt causes them to want you to be doing wrong as well.

The Bronner Company was growing fast, and Nathaniel was about to open a new store on Auburn Avenue when I realized something was wrong between him and my husband. Charles told me he and Nathaniel had a problem but would not tell me what it was. I would eventually find out years later. It was shortly after hearing about a problem that my husband told me he was writing his resignation from the Bronner Company.

I had mixed emotions about the whole thing. We were amidst a big celebration for the first brand new store that opened on Auburn Avenue when he turned in his resignation. I knew in my heart that the BB Company was going to be huge. What was wrong with my husband? He was utterly blind to the vision and the opportunity.

I was unhappy being away from my family and having to deal with my husband's change in attitude. It had stretched me to the point that I wanted to divorce him. I felt that I might have a better chance of staying in our marriage if we moved back to Philadelphia, so I did not protest his decision when he turned in his resignation. I asked many questions, but as usual, my husband made up his own story, which did not make sense to me.

He said he was having some problems and wanted to discuss them with Nathaniel, and at the time Nathaniel was busy preparing to open the new store and did not have time for him. Nathaniel told him that if he could not wait until after the grand opening celebration he could turn in his resignation. So, he decided to turn in his resignation.

I did not believe one word of that story but thought it best to leave it alone. There is usually some truth in most lies and I knew in time the real story would come forth.

Shortly after, he started working at the YMCA as a swimming pool attendant. I cracked up laughing when he told me what his job was because he could not swim. How can you be a swimming pool attendant who cannot swim? This could not have been good for his self-esteem. The job did not last. It was only a few weeks before the big newsflash came that we were leaving Atlanta.

It was an ordinary day and Charles had gone to work as usual. I did not suspect anything surprising or spectacular to happen that day, but before long he had returned home and seemed in a panic. He said to me, "We are leaving Atlanta," and I was speechless. I started to ask questions: "What happened? What is going on? When are we leaving?" He did not give me any sensible answers and I did not push him. It felt like we were being run out of town.

Due to our circumstances and what had happened, I knew it could not be anything positive that would cause us to leave in such a hurry. It only took a few hours to get packed and we were on our way with all our belongings in our new car. Most things belonged to our baby daughter, such as baby crib, stroller, swing, playpen and other paraphernalia. Polly and her husband were at work and I regret not being able to say goodbye to them. I did not realize how serious this move was until 42 years later. After doing a lot of investigating I learned the real reason we got out of Atlanta so fast. This information did not come easy, but I was relentless in my effort to know the truth about what really happened in Atlanta. Had I known the truth at the time it would have destroyed my marriage and my life.

CHAPTER FOUR

Back in Philadelphia

The trip back to Philadelphia was challenging. Charles had a problem following rules and driving was no exception. While going through a small town in South Carolina he was stopped for speeding. We were taken someplace where he was questioned and told that he would have to pay a fine. We did not have any money to pay the fine and they could not lock him up because they could not figure out what to do with the baby and me. After much discussion they told him he could leave his spare tire, they would hold it for collateral, and he could come back and get it when the fine was paid. It was completely bogus, and these country bumpkins just wanted some money. They settled on keeping the tire and we were on our way again.

Charles was careful about going through the small towns after that. Further up the road we had a flat tire and with no spare we had to have the tire fixed. It was a good thing the tire went flat near a service station and we were able to get it repaired. God protected us the rest of the journey and we arrived at 1436 Ogden Street safely.

I had mixed emotions about being back in Philadelphia. I felt like a failure had occurred in our lives and I was still in the dark about what happened in Atlanta. I was not happy living with my mother and father-in-law although my mother-in-law was very happy to have her son back. I felt some embarrassment returning to Ogden Street. My father and stepmother were still living across the street. It was odd that my father and stepmother had their first child, Denise, before I had my first daughter and later had a second daughter, Donna. It felt so weird to be having babies at the same time as my father.

Starting over was difficult. Living in my mother in law's house and having to follow her rules and take care of a baby was astounding. Before I left I had a decent job with the federal government and money in the bank, which made me feel independent. Returning with a baby, no job and no money reduced me to a very small denominator. Living on the third floor of a row home in North Philadelphia was not my idea or my dream of what I wanted in life. My husband also had a job with the federal government before we left. He was able to get another federal job soon after we returned at the Frankford Arsenal.

Working was not an option for me: one because my husband did not want me to work and two because I was pregnant every year for three years straight. My oldest daughter was born in Atlanta, on February 2, 1956. My second and third daughters were born in Philadelphia on May 4, 1957, and August 17, 1958. I would not have completed potty training for each before the other was born. Our goal was to buy a home with the money we had saved while we were engaged. The detour to Atlanta destroyed that. Now, we had to come up with another plan.

With only one of us working, it was difficult to save any money with three babies. Having completed our high school education in Philadelphia, my husband and I knew the importance of living in the better areas of the city for our children to go to the better schools. In other words, if you lived in an upscale neighborhood with or near the white people the schools would be rated higher and the education you received would be at the highest level with more opportunities.

We were determined to teach our children all we could and put them in the position to get the best education possible. I never talked to them about finishing high school. My words were, when you finish college. We loved our children and were eager to give them every opportunity for a better life through early childhood development, such as dancing, playing musical instruments, singing, going to summer camp, church and Bible study.

Learning to Drive a Car

After my third child, my husband informed me that I would have to learn how to drive so he would not have to take me and the children to the doctor each time we had to go. I was not interested in learning to drive a car. The thought made me nervous and afraid. I can't explain why it was so difficult for me. The first time my husband decided to teach me to drive the car was the most horrific experience.

One day without any warning or preparation he decided that he would teach me to drive, and he chose Broad Street for my first trial. When I sat behind the steering wheel I was shaking so bad my knees were out of control. I tried to hide my fear and listen and follow his instructions. I did what he said and managed to drive a short distance without having a stroke, or an accident. I did not want him to teach me but did not have a choice. The next lesson was in the park, which was much better. I wasn't so afraid because I was not in a lot of traffic like on Broad Street. I studied the driving manual and prepared for the driving test. I overcame the fear after a while and felt that I was ready to take the test at the driving test range.

Our car was not in the best condition at the time. I had managed to get to the stall where I was told to turn around and drive out. When I started the first turn the car stalled and I could not get it started. That was a failure of the driving part. My husband had to come and get the car out of the stall. I was overwhelmed with embarrassment, but I managed to answer all the questions correctly, so I only had to take the driving test over when I went back the second time. I practiced turning the car around in small spaces and was soon ready to take the test again and passed without any negative incidents. I am very grateful that my husband insisted I learn to drive, otherwise I may never have learned.

The Car Accident

In 1957 when my second oldest daughter, Kala, was three or four months old, our favorite cousins Juanita Bronner-Garmon and husband Roscoe, came from Atlanta to Philadelphia to visit us. It was an exciting time to be with them again. We had always enjoyed socializing together. Everything was going along swell and we decided to take them to visit Charles' sister Hazel Keels, who was living in Ambler, PA at that time with her husband and children. Juanita and Roscoe had driven to Philadelphia and Charles drove their car.

We arrived at Hazel's house safely and enjoyed our visit tremendously. On the journey home we were all feeling good and laughing and talking. Charles was driving, and I was seated on the passenger side of the car holding my baby in my arms. Baby seats were not required at that period. Seat belts were in the car but none of us had our belts fastened. Juanita and Roscoe were seated in the back of the car. We were headed east on Germantown Avenue returning home. Charles had a few alcoholic drinks as usual but we all felt that he was under control.

No one could imagine the freaky thing that was about to happen. We approached the curve on Germantown Avenue where the Trolley Car Diner stands today, just before the New Covenant Campus entrance. Charles was smoking a cigarette and the fire from it fell on to his lap. As he was looking down trying to brush the fire off he lost control of the car in the curve and ran straight into a light pole on the right side of the curve. I was looking at him as he was trying to brush the fire from his lap and did not see the accident coming. When the car hit the pole, I was catapulted into the dashboard while clutching my baby's head tight to my chest and hanging on to her. My baby was screaming, and I thought perhaps her head had hit the dashboard. Later I realized that my hands were bruised which had protected her head.

When the car stopped, we were asking questions of each other to determine if anyone was hurt. Juanita was the first one out of the car. I was so busy checking my baby I did not realize that I could not move. Juanita asked, "Lorene, are you and the baby alright? Charles, are you alright? Roscoe are you alright?" I was busy examining my baby, as she was yelling loudly, and did not realize that I was hurt. I could not see any physical harm to my baby, but when I tried to move, I could not. I was paralyzed from my waist down. Roscoe had received some bruises on his legs. Juanita and Charles did not seem to have any injuries.

When the police arrived, they took the report and accepted it as it happened. The emergency wagon crew put me on a stretcher to take me to the closest hospital, which happened to be Chestnut Hill Hospital.

When I arrived and was examined and X-rayed, they determined that I had a fractured pelvic bone. I would be admitted to the hospital and would take six weeks to recover. I was breastfeeding my baby and I could not imagine having to stop breastfeeding her and stay in the hospital for six weeks. I could not do anything but cry. My heart hurt along with my pain. My treatment was to be put into a body cast for six weeks. What and who is going to take care of my baby?

When I say body cast I mean just that. It was like a strait jacket. It started below my breast and covered me down to my knees, with an opening in the back and in the front for elimination and access. A wood bar went across the opening in the front for lifting. The first couple of weeks in this contraption were indescribable. I was miserable from head to toe. I could not be comfortable any way I tried. If I was lying on my back for any length of time I wanted to be turned onto my stomach. The nursing staff was very helpful, but they could not turn me as often as I needed. I had to eat my meals and do everything lying flat. I had strong medication for pain in the beginning but had to be taken off eventually for fear of becoming addicted.

After about two weeks of complete misery, I figured out how to maneuver myself to the edge of the bed holding on to the head of the bed and flip myself over. What a difference! I did not have to call for help. I was given medication to dry up my milk, but some of it had to be pumped out. It broke my heart that I would not be able to breast-feed my baby. After three weeks in the hospital, the pain had gotten better, and my medication was reduced. The doctors determined that I could go home to finish my healing and come back to the hospital when the six weeks were up and have the cast removed. Charles' Mother, Obie, had been helping him to take care of our two babies. Arrangements were made, and I was taken from the hospital by ambulance to his mother and father's house on Ogden Street.

Juanita's car was towed to a repair shop immediately following the accident and was repaired. They were able to drive back to Atlanta by the next weekend. The car was damaged in the front, but the motor was not harmed. Juanita, Roscoe and Charles visited me in the hospital before they went back home. I felt extremely sad that our wonderful time together had ended in such a strange and bizarre way.

Depression had taken hold of me and I was miserable. I blamed my husband for his carelessness.

When the six weeks were up I was taken back to the hospital and the cast was cut off. I had to learn to walk again. First using crutches and then a cane. After a few weeks of therapy, I was feeling good again. In a short period of time I discovered I was pregnant with my third oldest child, which caused me to be depressed again. I felt as though I was being attacked. I was concerned that having a baby shortly after a pelvic bone fracture might be too much to bear. Nine months later I had a healthy baby girl during a normal delivery, my third oldest child, Cheryl Darcel, later renamed Tauheedah. The first three years of my marriage I had three babies.

The Plan

As blacks gained better employment and started moving into white neighborhoods, the whites started moving out further into the suburbs. One example was when we bought our house in the section of the city called West Oak Lane, the block where we moved had two black families when we moved in. Five years later the whole block was black. This was in nineteen sixty-one. Our goal was to move from North Philadelphia into a better school district before our oldest daughter started kindergarten. We accomplished that goal, but it came with a price. Under our current circumstances we could not make such a move without the help of Charles' parents.

His mother wanted to move into a better neighborhood but needed help. He and his mom came up with the idea that we could find a house large enough for us to move together. They would provide the down payment and live rent free until the money was repaid. They would share the food and utility costs monthly. My husband was so selfish and did not consider my feelings at all. The conversation was brought up in front of both his parents and I was completely caught off guard. I did not agree but didn't know how to express my true feeling without hurting theirs. I liked his parents but did not want to live with them for an extended period.

Wanting the best for my children I felt trapped, with no money, no job, and three little children. I felt the sacrifice would be better than the alternative, so I agreed. Looking for a house brought some excitement into our lives, which was desperately needed. It did not take long before we found a four-bedroom house in an upscale neighborhood. It was conveniently located near a highly recommended elementary school (Howe School), and transportation to all parts of the city. When we went to look at the house I was amazed that we could smell the grass. The street was clean, and the neighborhood was quiet. The house was immaculate; freshly painted with hardwood floors. A new heater had been installed. The rooms were large and airy. This was the perfect house for us and we bought it.

The lawyer drew up the papers on our agreement and we went to settlement feeling good. The house was in our name: Charles U. Bronner and Lorene Bronner. The year was 1961. The house was located at 1448 W. Grange Avenue in a section of the city called West Oak Lane. One side of our block had some quaint stores. It is so ironic that we moved from the fourteen hundred block of Ogden Street to the same hundred blocks of Grange Avenue further north.

The house had four bedrooms, an enclosed porch, living and dining rooms, a breakfast room, kitchen, bathroom with stall shower and bathtub, and a full unfinished basement with toilet and garage. The front of the house had a yard where we planted bushes and flowers. Sometimes I planted tomatoes in the yard.

It was the beginning of a long relationship with his parents. The agreement between was that they would loan us the down payment which was two thousand dollars (the exact amount we had saved before we moved to Atlanta) and live without paying rent until the money was repaid.

We spent eleven years together before his parents decided to buy another house and move. For most of the eleven years, we got along well. We shared the responsibility of cleaning and cooking, buying groceries, and taking care of the children. Most of the work in the house was my job because I was home every day while everyone else was working on a job. I always had dinner ready when my husband and his parents came home from work. We ate our meals together and his mom and dad did the dishes. Charles' Mother enjoyed entertaining and she loved to cook. She was an excellent cook and would do all the cooking on weekends. We frequently had guests for dinner. Obie cooked large meals that always included dessert. Her favorite cakes were chocolate and pineapple.

It appears I was always pregnant, having a baby, miscarriage or abortion. My fourth daughter, Deanne Kimberly was born January 19, 1962 after we moved into our new home on Grange Avenue. Deanne was born at Albert Einstein Hospital on Broad and Olney Avenue. The hospital was within walking distance from our house.

It is very painful to write about the abortions that I had. I was so overwhelmed with being pregnant so many times I could not go through with them all. My husband had a solution for everything, so he suggested I go to Planned Parenthood and get help. In retrospect I don't recall him going with me either time. I remember the pain and shame that I felt during and after the experiences. I was counseled before and after and given protective devices to use.

Without my husband's cooperation the devices were of no use. He pretended that whatever I used for protection did not feel good and he would reject my using anything.

Because of his strong sexual desires and my desire to please him, I suffered the consequences of unscrupulous behavior. He was overly possessive and kept me isolated from my family as much as possible. Looking back on those years I realize it was a controlling factor and a form of abuse. He did not want me to visit my parents or my sister without him. By this time my father and mother had moved from across the street to a better neighborhood in North Philly. Submitting to my husband's selfish behavior would prove to be detrimental to me when I really needed family support. I am not saying that you should tell all your business to your family, but if you do not reach out and keep in contact it can be very difficult to ask for help when you need it.

Ignorance is so costly, and I am still paying for the times I allowed my husband to dictate to me and tell me lies. He had me believing that the baby was not formed until after 3 months, before that it was just cells and blood. I never discussed that part with my counselors. I believe now, as many do, that a baby is formed and is a human being at conception. The moment the sperm and female egg join, it is a person and to have an abortion is killing another human no matter what stage you are in. I am grateful that God let me live long enough to realize the sins of my youth, to be able to ask for forgiveness and know that I am forgiven.

After Deanne was born I became depressed and needed to do something for myself. I was always interested in doing hair and I enjoyed it, so Charles suggested that I attend Beauty Culture School to become a beautician. I needed something to get me excited about life again and was happy to start learning something new. I enrolled at HyStyle Beauty Culture

School, which was located at Broad and Thompson Streets. My daughter Deanne became a licensed beautician and teacher.

While attending school I became pregnant again with my fifth and sixth daughters (twins) born December 13, 1963, premature at seven months. My twins were a surprise to everyone including my doctor. I was so big that trying to wash the customer's hair while bending over the shampoo bowl at school was difficult. I felt something strange about this pregnancy that was different from all the rest. I told my doctor that something was wrong because I felt kicking all over my stomach, top bottom and sides at the same time. The doctor could not find anything wrong and did not hear but one heartbeat. Ultrasound was not being used or had not been discovered at that time.

My water broke at seven months and my husband rushed me to the hospital. I was very upset because I had never experienced an early delivery before. When I arrived at the hospital it was not long before the doctors discovered two heartbeats. The word spread quickly that I was having twins, which brought a lot of excitement to the delivery floor. I was upset and afraid that my babies may not live because it had only been seven months. In an effort to protect them, I was not given any anesthesia and had to deliver without the benefit of pain medication. It was a hard delivery and I screamed so loud as each one was born that I could only hear my scream and nothing else. One of my twins weighed 3 lbs. 11 oz. and the other weighed 3 lbs. 7 oz.

My worst fears were realized. They were identical girls and the one that weighed the most had a respiratory problem and only lived for several hours. My husband and I named them Lolita Lorene and Linda Lolene. Linda had to stay in the hospital until she weighed 5 pounds, which did not take but a few weeks. She had a good appetite and grew fast. My husband made all the arrangements for our Lolita to be buried at Rolling Green Cemetery in Chester, PA. While I was still in the hospital I was taken to the nursery and got to see them both. They were so precious and looked just like their father. I cried and prayed to God to let Linda live. It made me sad to have to leave her in the hospital and not be able to breastfeed her.

I visited Linda every day and held her and fed her at every visit until she weighed enough to come home. I was relieved and happy to have her home. When I felt strong again I went back to school and finished. Before finishing school, I was involved in a hair show. Barbara, my mother's half-sister, was my model. Her picture and my hairstyle were featured in a hair magazine. I kept the magazine for years until I gave it to an African Hair/Beauty Museum on 52nd Street in South Philadelphia. I felt very proud that I had done well enough for my style to appear in a magazine.

Something awful happened after that show. Linda was about two years old and I had missed my period but could not accept the fact that I was pregnant again, so I did nothing to care for myself and did everything to reject this pregnancy. I did not eat properly and did all kinds of stomach exercises, pushing and pulling on my stomach and whatever I could think off to make my period come.

Committing these acts did not seem wrong at the time because I was drowning and trying to save myself. Regardless of what I thought at the time, I was wrong and when you do wrong you suffer the consequences.

We were staying in a hotel downtown after a hair show and I started having severe cramps and thought my period was getting ready to come. I went to the bathroom and sat on the toilet feeling pressure from my rectum made it feel as though my bowels were about to move. I held my stomach and pressed on it to relieve the pain and a tiny baby came out into the toilet. I grabbed it quickly out of the water and was screaming and panicking for my husband to come, "Charles, Charles, come here!" He rushed into the bathroom asking what was wrong, "What happened?" I held the baby in my hand as I was crying uncontrollably.

"Look," I said, as I reached my hand out for him to see. The baby was so tiny, it fit into the palm of one hand completely formed. This was proof that a baby is a baby at conception when the egg and sperm come together. "Alright, calm down," was his reply as he helped me to the bed. The umbilical cord was still attached. I had six babies but had never seen any of them being born. The cord hanging from me attached to the tiny baby was a frightening sight. My husband helped me to the bed and called for help. He wrapped the baby and me in a towel and covered us with a sheet. An ambulance came and took me to the hospital.

I was given a treatment called a D&C, which means the uterus is dilated (opened) with an instrument and cleaned out. I was able to leave the hospital and return to the hotel. We did not talk about what happened to anyone. We checked out of the hotel when it was time and went home.

I was overwhelmed with grief for that tiny baby that I held in one hand. Knowing that I was responsible for its demise was too much to bear. I promised God that I would never do anything to destroy another life again and soon after I was put to the test.

A short time later I was able to take the State Board Test and get my Cosmetology License in 1966. I worked for a year in Dorothy's Beauty Salon, which was located in the 7200 block of Ogontz Avenue. I enjoyed the experience of working in a beauty salon but soon realized it was not my passion. I guess what made me know for sure it was not what I wanted to do was the fact that I became pregnant again with my 7th daughter Sonja Jean. When some of the customers knew that I was pregnant and did not want me to do their hair, I felt bad. I was so depressed until I could not stand to smell hair and did not want to do that work anymore.

Some old customers with old-fashioned ways thought that if a pregnant woman did your hair it would cause it to fall out. I guess it stemmed from slavery and old wives' tales. Whatever the case, I did not want to do hair. The other problem was morning sickness, which I had never experienced before. It was bad for about three or four months. I cannot explain the sick feeling that made me want to vomit but could not. I would lie on the floor sometimes, to try to get relief. I feel truly blessed that I only had to endure morning sickness with one pregnancy. I thought that maybe the morning sickness was because I was carrying a boy this time.

I had to do all my daughter's hair every day until they were old enough to do their own. My training paid off for me because I could do their hair and mine and did not have to go to a beauty salon. Before quitting work at Dorothy's Salon, I took part in another hair show contest in Philadelphia. My sister-in-law, Doris Manley, was my model. This was before Bronner Brothers started having hair shows in Atlanta. These shows in Philadelphia were held at the Sheraton downtown. Nathaniel Bronner Sr. attended these shows as well. My style did not make an impression with the photographer who was taking pictures and I was ignored. Nathaniel saw what was happening and asked the photographer to take pictures of my style, which he did. I never saw the pictures, and they were not in the magazine. I felt gratitude that Nathaniel complemented my hairstyle and appreciated my work.

Years later Dorothy sold her beauty salon and it is currently owned and operated by Cassandra. Also, who would have guessed that I would have a connection to that same beauty salon and the new owner, Cassandra, through my part-time job with Bronner Brothers Hair Care Company. I sold BB products, BB Hair Show tickets, and Upscale subscriptions to Cassandra and her staff in 2000.

CHAPTER FIVE

Eight Years of Crazy

In the 1970's black people in Philadelphia were moving into more affluent neighborhoods and white people were moving out into the suburbs. This change caused a shift that inspired many black men to buy businesses in the bar industry. Black-owned neighborhood bars started cropping up all over the place in the seventies but more so, in the West Philadelphia area.

In 1971 my husband decided to go into the bar business after his best friend, Randy Fisher, had bought a bar at 52nd & Stiles Streets in West Philadelphia called the Pony Trail. They both worked together at the Frankford Arsenal, a government agency in the northeast section of Philadelphia, for fourteen years. Randy told Charles that this was a great business to make money and be your own boss. Charles was looking for an easy way to make money and this seemed like a great opportunity. It was a turning point in the history of small neighborhood bars in Philadelphia when the white owners decided to sell and move out.

Charles bought the bar located at 59th and Nassau Streets, named the Nassau Inn. He renamed it Bronner's Lounge. The building was large and encompassed the whole corner of the quiet neighborhood street. You entered the bar from the basement on the ground level. You could access the first floor of the building from the front steps that led you to the porch area. There was a bedroom on the first floor, kitchen and ladies' bathroom, which was part of the business. The men's room was in the basement to the right of the entrance as you entered the bar. You could also enter the bar from a side door in the back of the building, which was used as an entrance for ladies. The room had booths for eating and drinking, and it was separated by a ramp that led from the bar area. You could not see the people in the back room unless you walked back there. From the back room, a few steps led you to the kitchen and ladies room. The kitchen was small but convenient to cook and serve food to the customers.

There was a separate entrance to an apartment on the second floor, which my husband rented to a couple. The apartment could be accessed from the front of the building with a separate entrance on the left. Another door to the right led to a bedroom that my husband reserved for himself. I had no knowledge of who rented the apartment, not knowing who they were or what they paid for rent. We had two mortgages, one for the bar business and one for the building. We had insurance on the mortgage loan that would pay it off in case of death.

The rooms on the first floor were part of the business, and the rooms on the second floor were part of the building loan, which was paid directly to the previous owners. They lived there and operated their business for many years. They told us that at one period women were not allowed in the bar area, but they could enter from the ladies' entrance on the side of the building and be served in the back room. The kitchen was small but had all the necessary equipment needed to serve food. It was only in operation from time to time. At one point, I cooked roast beef and served sandwiches. When the kitchen was in operation with a full-time chef, meals were available. The back room had comfortable booths to sit and eat.

Some other black bar owners my husband associated with were: Fat Albert's, located at 52nd & Girard; Little Willie's at 52nd & Lancaster Avenue; Charlie's Bar, in the 6100 block of Market Street; and Sid Booker's at Broad & Belfield Avenue. The Pony Trail and Sid Booker's are the only two bars that are still currently in operation. There were other blacks who were said to be 'fronting for the white man', which meant that the black person pretended to be the owner while working for the white man. My husband bonded with the real black owners and they supported each other. A group of owners formed an Association of Black Bar Owners to help one another.

Charles had a problem taking advice from anyone. He had a mind of his own and insisted on doing whatever his way. My name was on the deed as half owner of the business, but he did not listen to anything I had to say about the business. I tried to help by keeping the records and reporting to our accountant, so we would be able to keep up with taxes, social security, payments, mortgage payments and licenses for this and that. There were so many bills at the business and at home. It was not easy, and not being disciplined in all matters started to take a toll after about four years.

Small businesses encounter problems in maintaining good help, and that became increasingly difficult. Sometimes there was no one to attend the bar except my husband. Having to work both shifts, sometimes he asked me to help. I wanted the benefit of having a business, but this type of business was not my preference. I tried to stay away from it as much as possible. The bar business was not my cup of tea. This kind of business went against all my religious beliefs and I felt completely out of place. Still I was reminded of the days when I was young, working in my Grandfather Luviger's store in Alabama. I felt a sense of pride in being part-owner of a business regardless of the type. It was never my intention to physically work behind the bar. I could easily handle keeping the records and paying the bills.

Working in a bar was a new experience for me and it was not something I aspired to do. It was a shock to my personality, my religion, and my whole thought process and it took me a little while to get adjusted. I was never a full-time worker there but there were periods when the barmaid had been fired and someone had to do the job until a replacement could be found. I would fill in doing those periods, which were frequent at times. I could not understand how people could enjoy coming into a bar and sitting for hours talking and drinking liquor. It was not something that I enjoyed or wanted to do.

When you are drowning you reach for any means of survival. Acquiescing to this lifestyle was a means of survival for me if I was to help support my family and keep my husband. He did not want me to work but he didn't mind me working at the bar because he was practically always there and could keep an eye on me.

Another big adjustment for him was being in control of everything and everybody. Before the bar, he was getting paid every two weeks and doing fine. After he bought the business, he took the receipt money home every day. He had total access to money all the time and carried large sums in his pocket. His record keeping was outrageous. He would write checks and not keep a record of the amount or to whom it was written. I tried to keep accurate records of all monies for the accountant but to no avail. The whole process of operating the business was total chaos.

I will never forget my first time working behind the bar. I had no experience and had to learn as I went along. My husband showed me quickly how to pour a drink into a shot glass. I had observed the barmaids and how they did things, but you learn more by doing than by watching. My nervousness began to show when a customer asked for a drink with a twist of lemon. I did okay pouring the drink but when I squeezed the lemon it squirted into the customers' face.

I was petrified! "Oh, please forgive me, I am so sorry, I am new at this." The customer laughed at me and said, "Oh, its ok, don't worry about it, I know you did not do that on purpose." I wanted to disappear; the embarrassment was so overwhelming for me.

Wanting us to succeed, I was determined to help in whatever way I could. I acted as though I was another barmaid learning my job. My husband welcomed me being there when he needed help, but not so much when he didn't need me. I was ok with that until things began to spin out of control, and we had started to grow apart. His ideas and views of life no longer appealed to me.

I wanted to invest in a stable business like buying real estate. We had the opportunity to buy the houses on both sides of our house. The one house on the corner had a store and apartments over the top. The house on the other side had been converted into a duplex. I tried to convince my husband to buy the properties when they became available, but he did not agree.

Bronner's Lounge was in a quiet area in an upscale neighborhood, and most of our clients were professionals. They would meet every day after work just like the song, "Me and Mrs. Jones". My husband told me about the adult males in his family who would take him with them to see other women in his early years of growing up. He developed a very cynical attitude toward women and believed that all women would cheat. This attitude was so embedded in him until it made him extremely jealous and not trusting of any women.

He never trusted me and was always accusing me of cheating with every man who showed any friendship toward me. Because he was cheating on me he could not imagine that I was not cheating also.

It was not in my DNA to be a cheater. I was a one-man woman, totally in love with my husband, and I did not want any other man. Being totally naïve and trusting everyone made me a target, suspected of doing wrong when I was innocent. I did not believe that people would think bad of you or lie on you for no reason. I believed that if I treated everyone the way I wanted to be treated that I would be liked and respected for it. That is not the case. People will lie on you because they are jealous of you and want what you have. It took me a long time to get it, but I finally did.

Also, there were times when my husband had made a mess of things at the bar and needed me to take over for a while. He would stay away until I got things in order and he would return and take over again. Even though he needed help it was difficult for him to relinquish his power. As time went on he incurred gambling debts and borrowed from a loan shark who happened to be our neighbor. The interest rate was outrageous! And he was in way over his head. I learned about the ordeal after everything was spinning out of control. He could not pay the loan shark, so he decided to let him work behind the bar. He paid the debt with whatever he could spare from the proceeds of the day and also paid him for working. It was the craziest thing I had ever witnessed.

This went on for several months but as I asked more questions and got some truthful answers I realized that it would take a long time to pay the debt off because of the high rate of interest and the large sum that was owed. During this period, our house mortgage was getting further and further behind. The utility bills at the bar were not being paid and business was in a slump. To make matters worse, I became pregnant and had a miscarriage. I was on an emotional roller coaster, pregnant, afraid of losing my house and the business. I figured I had already lost my husband because he had been in a rehab for alcohol abuse, and he came out and told me he would never stop drinking. At one point, I went to the mortgage company to try to save our house from foreclosure. He did not go with me but afterward he was able to work out a deal with them.

My husband was out of control in many areas. One day while we were alone in the bar for a brief period he told me he had a son in Atlanta. I became irate and started screaming at him like a crazy woman. My husband was such a liar but when I looked closely at the things he said I could always find some truth in his stories. As soon as the words came out of his mouth I started threatening him. "Oh, you have a son, where is he? What's his name? When did you get him? If you have a son and I find out that its true, you can go to hell and forget about me because I will be gone out of your life." I guess I convinced him to stop the conversation because he did not say anymore.

The incident created some serious thoughts about our stay in Atlanta and the possibility that he could be telling the truth. I had to let it go for the time being but was determined to find out if it was true. I started to investigate years later. I wanted to know the truth but did not know if I could handle the truth. Still I kept searching.

My Change of Heart

After many unusual and embarrassing moments at the bar that affected me deeply, I had a change of heart. One example that was unforgettable was a night that I was at the bar, not working but socializing with the customers as I did on a limited basis. My husband was watching as I had a conversation with a male customer. Nothing unusual happened, no touching, in full view of everyone, sitting opposite each other at a small table. Suddenly, my husband approached us and told me to come to the back room.

I felt some uneasiness as I followed him but could not imagine what was about to happen.

We sat down in the booth and he started questioning me about the conversation I was having with the male customer. The man had not shown any disrespect to me and I told him that. His fist came into my forehead like a rushing wind that catches you off guard and nearly knocks you down. I would have fallen if I had not already been seated. A humongous swelling popped out on my forehead and I was crying and asking him why he hit me when I was not doing anything wrong. One of his friends, who was also a Mason brother from his lodge, came in the back and saw what had happened. When he saw my face, he said, "Man, what did you do? Man, you are wrong!" He gave me some tissues to wipe my tears and clean my face. Charles did not respond. I was grateful that no one else from the front of the bar saw or knew what happened.

The embarrassment was overwhelming, and I wanted to disappear. I was starting to look like a monster from the swelling and discoloration of both eyes. It was a blessing that I had the opportunity to go out the back-side entrance without being noticed. I had money from the day's receipts and I walked from Nassau Road to Lancaster Avenue and caught a cab to go home. Charles was unapologetic; he said nothing when I said I was going home. If he had any remorse for what he did I was not made aware of it.

The next day I went to the Einstein Hospital to have my eyes checked. I wore dark glasses for weeks and stayed at home for months, waiting for my black and blue eyes to clear up. Fortunately, I did not sustain any damage to my eyesight; only my self-esteem was severely damaged. I don't recall his mother or father asking me any questions about my face during the entire period it took for my face to clear up.

I am sure they knew it was his doing because they both had witnessed it happen in the kitchen of their home after we returned from Atlanta.

I was nine months pregnant with my second daughter, Kala, when Charles punched me in the face in full view of his parents. He became upset with me about something I said that did not agree with him. His Mother screamed at him to stop but the damage had already been done. His father did not say a word. A few days later I went to the hospital to deliver Kala with a black eye. My father came to see me and was very upset. This led him to threaten Charles, warning him to never lay hands on me again. From the first time my husband hit me in the face to the second time, thirteen years had passed, and I was shocked, completely caught off guard. I didn't think he would ever do that again.

He never apologized when he did wrong but would go to extremes being extra nice, like buying me gifts and taking me places that he knew would make me feel good again. I would try to punish him by ignoring him and not talking for as long as possible. He would stay overnight at the bar in his private room when we were not getting along well. When we were doing well I would stay with him from time to time. My life during this crazy eight was like being on a roller coaster, depending on which personality would show up in my husband. Would he be the fun-loving, easy going, loving father? Or would he be the disgruntled strict disciplinarian? The one who stayed in bed most of the day and asked to be waited on?

At this stage, drinking alcohol was more in control of who showed up. He had the ability to stop drinking for periods of time, which could be a few weeks, but he was not the same. During these periods he would isolate himself and stay in bed while depending on me to operate the business. He would knock on the bedroom floor for the children to bring him food or drink to our bedroom. As much as I wanted him to stop drinking alcohol, I liked the alcoholic Charles better than the sober one.

My black and blue eyes were opened to the need to do something different. Cosmetology was not it anymore. I wanted to go back to working in an office where I felt the most comfortable. I kept my State License current for many years in case I would decide to work in the beauty industry again. By this time, I had lost all my office skills and needed to learn how to type on an electric typewriter and learn shorthand. I had experience on a manual typewriter before and computers were in the future. I did not have any money for school, so I was fortunate to learn of the Opportunities Industrialization Center (OIC) founded by Rev. Dr. Leon Sullivan.

It was a free training program for low-income and underprivileged people like me. I was accepted into the Stenographer-II Program. Being in this program gave me the opportunity to meet some influential, outstanding people, like Rev. Melvin Floyd, M.Ed., then 46-year Urban Missionary and Soul Winner since 1966. During my training at OIC, a few students including myself had the opportunity to work in Rev. Floyd's office for a short time. It was a great experience working with him in such a clean calm environment.

Another very special individual was State Representative David P. Richardson Jr. who was elected at the age of 24 to represent Pennsylvania's 201st Legislative District. I had not met or heard of David before my friend, Esther Solomon, who was also my classmate, told me that he was going to speak to our class. I asked, "Who is David Richardson?" "You are going to love him," she said. "He is a true brother and a champion for all the people." She was absolutely right.

What I didn't know was Esther was a good friend of David and his family. She had asked David to come and speak to our class, and he did not disappoint. A few years later he was the keynote speaker at my youngest daughter Sonja's graduation from high school. David was very supportive of my daughters and of me, and Sonja asked him if he would speak at her graduation. He was an eloquent speaker and said things to inspire and motivate people to want to love others and help one another. He was never negative and did not say anything bad about an individual. If he could not say something good, he would not say anything at all and would not participate in the conversation if you were talking negatively about someone. I got to know him from the many times we had dinner at Esther's house after she and I became close friends.

After graduation, Esther and I both became employed. She with the Pennsylvania State Department and I with a private grant program that was dependent on funding to keep going. It only lasted a year until the funding ran out. Sometimes, I would make extra money styling wigs in my home. My husband was operating the Bar on his own. The money I made was spent on our children and whatever I needed for myself. My biggest regret during that period was my inability to save money.

I also did part-time work at Christmastime at Lord & Taylor, located in Jenkintown on Old York Road. I usually worked only during the holidays but one time I worked until the Spring. This was an enjoyable experience for me.

Starting as a cashier and gift wrapper, I was promoted to a salesperson in the coat department and given an opportunity to stay and work full-time. I only stayed from Christmas until April before I resigned. During this time, I met my friend Elsie Benn, who was also a cashier, and discovered we were both members of the Nazarene Baptist church. Our friendship grew, and she was like a sister until her demise.

A Very Rough Time

My husband, our children and I lived together peacefully with his mom and dad for approximately fifteen years without any major problems. His mom and I shared the cooking, cleaning, and grocery shopping. The major part of cooking and cleaning was my responsibility because everyone else had a job except the children. As the children grew older and developed their own personalities, things changed in terms of them having friends and playing loud music and so on, which made a different atmosphere in the house. It was probably disturbing to Charlie and Obie.

Obie started to change and one day while we were in the kitchen she started to talk about her husband in a way I had never heard her speak about him. She started the conservation like, "You know Charlie is something. He will go with anybody. I found some letters from some woman in his drawer." I did not know how to respond. I had no clue as to what he would or would not do, or if he was involved with anyone. So, I said, "Really? I didn't know that." "Yes," she said and added that it didn't matter to him who it was, it could be family, and he would mess around with anyone.

I was speechless and did not want to hear that nonsense. My mind was struggling to know what to say. I had never experienced anything dishonest about my father-in-law and did not believe the things she was saying. I respected them both and did not feel that kind of negativity about either of them. I thought we had a mutual respect and they treated me like a daughter and I felt very close to them. In my mind' struggle I was wondering, "Where is she going with this? What is her problem? What does she want from me?"

The questions came like a flood, but no answers came to let me know what to say to her.

A few days later the answer was revealed in the form of a big blowout! I had gone down in the basement to wash clothes and shortly after Charlie came downstairs to get something and he went back up. A few minutes later I heard some loud talking which sounded like he was being accused of something. When I came upstairs Obie was waiting for me in the dining room. She was in a rage and started ranting and asking me questions. "What are you and Charlie doing? Why does he have to follow you every time you go in the bathroom or downstairs in the basement? You must be leaving notes for each other." I was in shock with my mouth wide open and at a loss for words. When my words did come out they were loud and angry.

By this time my husband Charles had heard the commotion and came downstairs. When I could speak I had more questions than answers, "Are you crazy? What do you think I want with an old man? I do not cheat, and I have never cheated. I have your son, so what do you think I want with your husband? You must be cheating so you accuse me of doing the same." I don't know if she was trying to make me say I was cheating, but she said, "Yes, I cheat." My answer was, "Well I don't."

My husband stood still and did not defend or accuse but told me not to talk to his mother like that. I was outraged that he would say that to me after she had totally disrespected me, and herself.

I cannot explain what that episode did to me. All my trust and respect and love for my mother-in-law dissipated that day and I could not ever feel the same about her. Our relationship changed forever and the shocking effect it had on me was unbelievable. I could not sleep after that and had to seek help from a psychiatrist at Einstein Hospital. Thank God it only took one visit. I don't remember his name, but he was very convincing. He asked me, "Why are you worried about what your mother-in-law thinks? You should not let what she thinks bother you. You know the truth. Does your husband believe you?" My answer was "Yes," because he did not accuse me.

The doctor said, "That is all that's important that he trust and believe you." Something clicked inside of my brain and I thought, "You are absolutely right. That woman is crazy. I will know how to treat her from now on. She will be treated with a long-handled spoon." That one visit was enough for me. I was disappointed and hurt but I managed to go on and treat her kindly. We didn't have much conversation from that time forward and we avoided each other as much as possible. Only conversing when it was necessary.

Shortly after that, she and her husband bought another house and moved to Mount Airy. Our relationship was never the same, but I treated her with respect. I refused to let that incident interfere with her relationship with my children. They loved their grandmother and had a very good relationship with her. I did not see the point in destroying what they had together.

My husband and I did not talk about it anymore after I saw the psychiatrist. I continued to attend family dinners on Thanksgiving and Christmas at my mother and father-in-law's house or when relatives from out of town would come and visit. My husband would leave the bar and go to his mother's house instead of coming home, which was like what happened in Atlanta. I was very happy when his parents moved because for the first time I could make decisions without consulting with her.

I thought my husband and I would get a closer relationship and really enjoy our home for real. Imagine my disappointment when I was exposed to the same old behavior from him that I had already tolerated for long enough. I did not talk against her to my children and they each developed their own personal relationships with their grandmother and grandfather.

I did not tell my children what happened until they were grown, and their grandmother had passed away. I kept thinking at some point in time before she died she would admit she was wrong about me and apologize, but it did not happen.

Charles Joins the Masonic Lodge

One day my husband was in a very good mood; with a lot of excitement he told me he was going to become a member of a Masonic Lodge. I was excited for him because I remembered my Grandfather Luviger was a member of a Masonic Lodge in Alabama. I believed it to be a secret organization that did some good things.

Shortly after opening his business my husband began to make new friends and some of them were members of King David Lodge #52. He was very interested in becoming a part of this distinguished group of men, so he applied and was accepted. His affiliation began in February 1973. He was a member of King Solomon Chapter No. 1 and Demolay Consistory No. 1. One of his best friends Randy Fisher was also a Mason in another lodge. My knowledge of what the Masons did was limited to the affairs that my husband took me to, such as formal balls, banquets, cabarets and awards dinners. He attended meetings and paid dues, but never really gave me any details of what they did at the meetings or what the philosophy of the organization was.

There were times when I felt he should have spent more time being concerned about his business rather than the Masons' business. Charles was acting very strange one day while we were alone in the business and he asked me, "If I die will you let the Masons do their ritual before the funeral service?" I laughed and asked him, "Why are you asking me such a silly question? Are you planning on dying anytime soon?" He let me know that he was serious, and I responded by saying, "Of course I will." When I realized how serious he was I became frightened, and the thought came to mind that this could be a premonition. I rejected that horrible thought and changed the subject.

King David Lodge #52

(Excerpt from The History of King David Lodge #52 Revised and Updated by P.M. Kevin L. Myers, Jan. 15, 2003).

"King David Lodge #52 was warranted as a Lodge on December12, 1872. At the end of 1873 King David Lodge #52 had grown to thirty-one Financial Brothers. In 1882, King David Lodge, like many other lodges, was represented at the Masonic Convention to unite the two Grand Lodges that was held on December 26, 1882; A.L. 5882.

The representatives were: W.M. Bro. Frank Brunnick, S.W. Levon Henry & J.W. John B. Parker. After the installation of the new Most Worshipful Grand Master Bro. William H. Miller, he proceeded to appoint his Officers for the ensuing year. Among them were several of King David's brothers; namely, Bro. George A. Fassett as Senior Grand Deacon and Bro. Isreal Purnell as Senior Grand Steward. King David Lodge #52 has produced three Most Worshipful Grand Masters: They were: Bro. George A. Fassett, 1898-1899, Bro. Phillip H. Edwards, 1912-1913, Bro. Henry M. Baysmore, 1962-1963.

"There are several brothers that have rendered long and distinguished service to the lodge in official capacities for more than 30 years. These include: Past Master Sinkler A. Casselle; as Treasurer, Past Master Otho H. Halliburton and Master Mason Little B. Tyler; who both served as Financial Secretary. Brother Charles Albert Tindley, renowned Pastor of the great Tindley Temple United Methodist Church, 750 South Broad Street was a member of King David Lodge #52. He was one of the truly great ministers of his time.

"King David Lodge #52 contributed financially when the First Masonic District was interested in buying the Temple at 17th & Diamond Streets. Annual donations are given to our adopted School. The lodge has cultivated lasting fraternal relationships that have turned into adoptions. King David Lodge has always been known for its ritualistic work. We had, at one time, a traveling Degree Team that performed all ceremonies of the Ritual. We would sojourn across the Commonwealth when called upon to assist other lodges with their work. King David Lodge #52 produced another Most Worshipful Grand Master, Joseph B. Jefferson, in 2015."

My Part-Time Job

About four years into the eight years of crazy, I began to dislike our lifestyle and did not feel comfortable living it. I was at the business too much and felt that my children were being neglected. Charles' Mom and Dad were still with us at that time which helped.

My sister, Claudia Munford, joined the World Book Encyclopedia Company in 1970, the year before my crazy eight started. It is so ironic that our friend Naomi Jones, who was a District Manager at the time, recruited her into the company, the same Naomi that would play a significant role in my life in 1979.

I needed a set of encyclopedias for my children and could not afford to buy them. My sister convinced me to sell the books and I could earn a set. It sounded good and it would also help me to have some money so that I did not need to ask my husband. He provided well, but I did not like the fact that I had to ask him for every penny and tell him what I needed it for. It made me feel like a child asking my parent.

I set up appointments at my convenience. At that time, we were trained to go from door to door selling the books, in addition to making phone calls and setting up appointments. That part of the job was very challenging for me. I did not like going to someone's door and asking them to buy a set of encyclopedias. When I started the door to door I would knock or ring the bell and pray that no one would answer the door. I was never alone during my training, but it did not take the fear away. I would give a beautiful demonstration and be afraid to ask the customer to buy the books. Most of my sales came from people who were looking to buy a set of encyclopedias and did not need to be convinced.

My sister Claudia quickly moved up the ladder and became an Area Manager in 1973, a District Manager in 1976, a Division Manager in 1980 and a Branch Manager in 1987. Claudia was the first black woman to have been promoted to Branch Manager in the history of the World Book Company. She held the position in Middlesex, New Jersey and was very successful until she retired.

My sister recruited me into the company in 1975 and always worked hard to help me improve my skills, but I did not have what it takes to really succeed at selling anything. Despite my shortcomings, over a period of fourteen years I experienced some growth, became a District Manager, and in 1989 I was awarded a trophy for top District Manager in our branch.

I made some money and enjoyed meeting new people, going on trips, attending luncheons and dinners and receiving lovely unique gifts from the company. My children became recipients of sets of encyclopedias for their children from my efforts. I have many cherished gifts that I use today, i.e. crystal plates and glasses, classic books, encyclopedias, and a 2-volume set of the Presidents of the United States.

The best gift of all was the opportunity to work with my sister and meet so many lovely people who through the years have remained my friends, a few are: Celeste Mumford, Rev. Dr. Thelma Prescott, Grace McCullum, Dora Hardy, Mary Calloway, Ollie Carson and Gwendolyn Duncan. The company that we worked for is no longer in business, but it was an excellent company to work for. We had the opportunity to travel many places that I had only dreamed about. Wherever we traveled our accommodations were always First Class. We always stayed in the best upscale Hotels and only dined in the best restaurants wherever we traveled. My first trips were with World Book, traveling to the Pocono Mountains, Chicago, Miami, Hawaii, Freeport in the Bahamas, Pennsylvania Dutch Country and others too numerous to mention.

CHAPTER SIX

A Day I'll Never Forget

It was a cold and wretched day, December 23, 1978; a day that has been branded on my brain and will not go away. We had chosen to do our Christmas shopping on the 23rd but first had to take my husband to his business because he didn't have his car. The night before, he had taken his five-year-old grandson, Tony, out to spend some quality time together. On the way home, his car broke down on a bridge. That was strange because he had a good car that had never broken down before. Of course, there were no cell phones back then, so he had to walk a long distance to get to a telephone.

He reached a phone and called our third oldest daughter, Cheryl, to come and get them. Cheryl was eager to get them because it was freezing cold and little Tony must have felt much like an icicle. When they arrived home that night, another strange thing happened. As Charles was getting out of the car, he accidentally fell on the ice. It was good he had not hurt himself. The next day he was without transportation as the car had to be towed to the auto shop and repaired.

That morning as we were leaving to go Christmas shopping with my sister Claudia, Charles asked, "Would you pick me up when you finish your shopping?" He spoke with such sadness in his voice that I can't explain, and a look on his face of total defeat. My reply had an annoyed tone as I said, "You don't have to stay here all day; when you finish taking care of the business you can get a cab or someone to take you home."

"What time are you coming back? You can pick me up when you finish shopping," he said. I told him that I didn't know what time we would be finished. We had a lot of shopping to do and my sister was going with us. "We will probably be in the stores until closing," I said, "so, why don't you get a cab and go home, there is no need for you to stay here drinking all day. I will call to see where you are when we get finished. If you are still here we will pick you up." I spoke in a very frustrated tone of voice because I couldn't hide my true feelings. You could always tell when something was not right with me in my facial expression and my voice.

The next time I spoke to my husband we were at my sister's house sorting out our packages. When he called it sounded as though he was having a panic attack. He said, "Where are you? Why have you taken so long to call? I have been waiting here all day for you to pick me up!" As usual he did not take my advice and go home. He was extremely agitated and said, "I want to go home." I told him we would be there soon. Our daughter Cheryl spoke to him in a gentle tone and reassured him that we would be there soon, and she also told him she loved him.

I was so infuriated with him, I could hardly respond. "I am at my sister's house and as soon as we finish getting her things out of the car we will be on our way to pick you up." I will never forget the angry words I spoke after I hung up the phone. "That pain in the ass is still at the bar. Why didn't he go home like I told him to?"

Cheryl and I hurried to get our packages separated from my sister's, so we could get into the car and go to get my husband. It took about twenty-five minutes to get to the bar. When we arrived, it looked like a Hollywood Movie scene. The lights were on outside the building and Police Cars were all around. We were in shock. "Oh my God what happened," were my first words. Whatever it was I knew it was bad. My daughter became hysterical and could not park the car.

One of our customers, who was also a friend, came out and told us something bad had happened, and he parked the car for us.

We walked into the bar with fear in our hearts. As we introduced ourselves to a police officer at the door, and I asked what happened, the officer said, "Your husband has been shot and he is at Lankenau Hospital." "Is he alright," I asked?" "It's bad," was all I heard. I knew the few people who were there because they were regular customers. I searched each face and asked if he was alright. The only response I got was "It's bad."

I asked the Policeman to take us to the hospital and he was gracious enough to do so. 'It's bad' did not mean much because people get shot every day and live to be old. We had only gone a short distance from the bar when an announcement came over the policeman's car radio very clearly stating that a homicide had been committed at 59th and Nassau Streets, which is the address to our business.

My daughter was crying out loud and I was holding her in my arms trying to console her, so she did not hear the report. Oh No! No! No! This cannot be real: my heart was pounding, and my head felt like it was going to explode, full of fear and disbelief I asked myself, could this mean that he is dead? Did I really know the definition of homicide? This had to be some foul and ominous nightmare that felt like I was in the pit of hell. Surely, I am going to awaken, and my husband will be lying beside me in bed.

Premonition Turned Reality

The only way this could be real – I would have to see him with my own eyes. When we arrived at the hospital, the doctor that greeted us tried to prepare us as best she could.

She told us he had been shot in the head and died immediately, and that he did not suffer. She also said that his face is swollen, and he may not look like himself, and she offered us a sedative. I refused because I knew that whatever I had to face I needed a clear head, to manage my broken heart. I just thanked her politely and asked to see my husband.

When we walked into the area where he was we were shocked beyond belief that it was him lying there with a gunshot wound to the head, swollen face, blood running from his nostrils and one eye sunken in. My daughter and I held on to each other and cried at this horrific sight. It could not have been more than an hour before that I had talked to him on the phone with an annoyed voice that I wished I could take back.

"Oh my God, what am I going to do?" My mind was racing as I looked at him in disbelief. I was alone with two children in college, one in high school and one in elementary school. My bills were out of control. My house mortgage was four months delinquent. The electric bill at the bar was one thousand dollars. Those were just a few of the things that clouded my mind immediately, plus the fact that I was late sending the insurance payment on the policy that would pay the mortgage off on my house. It was enough to give me a splitting headache. We had acquired a second mortgage on the business loan and did not buy insurance to cover the loan as we had on the first mortgage. The other recently purchased life insurance that was less than two years old left a question in my mind. I felt numb, but my mind was racing as the Police officer drove us back to the bar.

What about the pending divorce? I had not shared my filing for divorce with anyone. Enough time had elapsed that I could be divorced. My mind raced: "Oh, my God, what if the divorce went through? Call your lawyer first thing in the morning. Send off the insurance payment as soon as you can. Get to the post office." I had many more questions than answers. The divorce decree had been sent to my husband about two months prior to his death but he chose to ignore it. He never spoke to me about it. I saw the papers lying on the top of the bureau in our room, so I know he received it. We were both doing what we always did, keeping our problems to ourselves.

Everything seemed normal on the surface. I continued to act as though nothing was going on. From all outward appearances, nothing had changed. We were still sleeping together and treating each other kindly. I had not shared with anyone that I was getting a divorce. We did not discuss our problems with our children or any other family members. I was not going to change that and tell this to anyone either. Through our 23 years of marriage, I did not discuss our problems with family and friends.

At one point, I considered counseling and did go to one session, but it was too late for me. Counseling may have helped if it had been done when it was first needed. The questions kept bombarding my mind, "What should I do now?" I must notify the family, call his mother, my sister Claudia, his sisters, and they can tell the others. It was after midnight by this time and I had to return to the bar and close it up in addition to trying to find out what happened and why.

The policeman took us back to the bar and a few people were still there including the barmaid who had worked with us for almost eight years. She looked as though she was in shock. I asked her what happened, and she replied, "Three black men came into the bar to rob him and when he resisted they shot him and took the money and ran out of the bar. The police were called immediately but by the time they arrived the men had disappeared." None of the eyewitnesses could identify these men.

My sister Claudia and her husband Tommy came to the bar as soon as they were informed, also Charles' friend, Randy Fisher came and offered his support. What happened was so unbelievable it was like we were amid a bad dream and had not awakened. We were up all-night crying and trying to figure out why and how this could happen. It was two days before Christmas on December 23, 1978. Normally we would have been happy getting ready to celebrate the birth of Jesus Christ, but there was nothing normal about this time. It would be many years before I would be able to get through the Christmas holidays without feeling extreme sadness and remembering the tragedy we suffered.

Our cousin Willie Maddox came to our house the day before Christmas with a Christmas tree that he decorated for us because none of us had the interest, energy or inclination to do anything. Part of me had died and I thought the rest of me was going to follow. What would have been a celebration had turned into devastation and high blood pressure, which was my diagnosis shortly after my husband's demise. Many neighbors came and offered their condolences, but what was most memorable was a full-course meal prepared and delivered to me by my neighbor, Susie Averette and her daughters, Diane, Carol, Debbie and Claudia.

Funeral arrangements were made, and the service was held on December 27, 1978 at Holsey Temple CME Church located at 5305-15 Germantown Avenue where Charles had become a member during his youth. A huge crowd showed up. My Pastor, Rev. Cherry, and Mrs. Cherry came and gave condolences. The Masons did their ritual and I felt good about honoring my husband's wishes. This handsome young man lying dead in a casket was not the ending to our twenty-three years of marriage that I had envisioned. A divorce would not stop me from communicating or loving him. He was the father of all my children without a doubt.

The whole family was shaken beyond explanation. My youngest daughter Sonja, who was nine years old, gave a beautiful talk about her father at the service. Overwhelming sadness prevailed over a service that was done decently and in order on Wednesday night, December 27, 1978. Burial was the next morning at 9:30 a.m. at Rolling Green Memorial Park, West Chester.

It felt like the coldest day of the year and the wind was fierce and unrelenting, which made me think I would literally freeze before leaving the cemetery. In addition, my mind was racing with thoughts of what now? I must go back home alone and figure out how to handle this business that did not fit my personality.

It was very difficult to open the business again, but realizing I had to continue and try to sell the business, I kept moving forward. One of our customers who lived on the same block offered to clean the bar for me. I cannot remember his name, but he was an angel. It was distressing to watch him mop my husband's blood from behind the bar where he had fallen, after being shot in the head. He did an excellent job, as I was grieving in silence and trying not to show how scared I was.

When I opened back up, one of the first unpleasant things I had to do was to fire one of the barmaids. I had never fired anyone in my life and it was a difficult task that I was unprepared for. I prayed and asked God to give me the words to say and for the young woman to accept my decision without any hassle. We had a civil conversation and she admitted I had a legitimate reason to fire her.

Six Months of Despair

After returning to reality, I experienced some emotional negatives that were hard to endure. I was very lonely and afraid. I have always been very private about my marriage and personal affairs, which had not changed because of the circumstances. I had to decide what to do with the business. I kept it operating with the same hours, always opening and closing at the same times. Business was not the same and many customers who were regulars did not frequent the bar as before. The income had decreased significantly for the day and night shifts. I was not able to be there all the time but had people to help me. What was a thriving, lucrative business was no more.

Some strange things began to happen during that time. One day a customer came in sat at a table by the mirrored wall and took his elbow and smashed it into the mirror. He was talking to himself as if he was insane. Another time someone went into the men's room and broke the toilet. I felt as though someone was trying to give me a message to get out. I told Randy about my mixed emotions and he was in total agreement with me to sell because he agreed that this type of business did not fit my personality. In retrospect, I could have shared with him the dire straits that I was in and asked him to help me determine a good price to sell the business. I know he would have given me sound advice, but my pride would not let me share and I suffered the consequences. Instead of asking people that I trusted, I contacted the real estate agent that sold us the business and trusted the accountant.

The Trip that Helped Save Me

From working with the World Book Encyclopedia Company, I had won a trip to Hawaii. It was scheduled for January 1979.

My husband was gunned down in December 1978. This trip was a gift that helped me to be able to move forward.

I had less than a month to prepare for this trip and a zillion things to do. With Randy Fisher's help, I could pull it off. He volunteered to take charge of the business for the entire week I was away. Despite the fact that he had his own business to run, he did all the necessary things to keep my business operating. This trip gave me the opportunity to rest and regroup. I believed it saved me from becoming ill from all the stress. The beauty of Hawaii made me feel a closeness to God that I had not experienced before. I could enjoy the activities of the day and sleep well at night.

My roommate was a white woman that I did not know. It was okay because we were on two different schedules. She came in late every night after I had gone to bed and left early every morning before I got up. We had no communication, which was fine because I did not want to talk anyway. It was as if I had a room to myself. This unique situation gave me an opportunity to sleep, pray, meditate, and plan what to do with the rest of my life. I spent the days with my sister Claudia, her husband Tommie and her son Bryan, and other friends from our group.

There were co-workers from different areas of the country; some of them were friends who had traveled with us before. We spent a week in Honolulu and stayed in the beautiful Waialua Hotel. This hotel was always shown at the beginning of the TV show called Hawaii Five-O in 1979.

My oldest daughter Deborah and her husband Tyrone were both in the Armed Service at the time and stationed in Hawaii. They took us to their apartment, sightseeing, shopping and dinner. It was a pleasure spending time with them.

One of the most exciting things we did was visiting the Polynesian Cultural Center. It was so beautiful, and they put on an exciting show. I have always been amazed at the dancers swaying their hips so effortlessly. The dinner boat ride was the greatest and I could dance with my nephew Bryan and really enjoy it. My mind got to rest for a week. When I returned, I could fight again. Things seemed to have gone well while I was away. Randy went over the receipts and explained everything to me. I was satisfied with what he had done and grateful for his support.

Selling Bronner's Lounge

Psalm 16:18-19: Pride goes before destruction, and a haughty spirit before a fall. Better to be of a humble spirit with the lowly, than to divide the spoil with the proud.

This scripture came to mind when I was in the process of selling Bronner's Lounge. Gripped with fear from all sides my pride would not allow me to share my dire circumstances with my family, and this led me to make some bad decisions. As close as my relationship was with my sister I never told her about my personal circumstances. I did not ask anyone to help me with the sale of the business and I did not tell Charles' mother or father what the situation was. I had not mentioned the divorce to them either. Having not shared before, my pride would not allow me to share it now.

The bills were out of control at my home and the business. I didn't know who to trust and didn't trust anyone. I was suspicious of everyone that came near me, especially black males. I would ask myself, "Could this or that one be the ones who murdered my husband? What if those men would come back again?" I was told three black males came into the bar and shot my husband in the head and took whatever money was in the cash register. It was an act of terror and beyond comprehension three days before Christmas. The one person I turned to was a close friend and former co-worker of my husbands, Randy Fisher. He was an honest person and was like part of my family. He would always support my husband. That same night he came to my home and offered to assist me in whatever way he could. I welcomed his support but could not tell him my true circumstances.

The first thing on my agenda was to send in the monthly payment on a life insurance policy that was late. I only had two insurance policies, one was to pay off the balance on the house mortgage and the other was a five-thousand-dollar straight life, which wasn't two years old. I learned that if a life insurance policy was less than two years the insurance company can decide to give you your money back rather than pay if they find any discrepancy on the application. They did find that my husband had been in a facility that treats alcoholics but, on the application, his answer was no to the question. I acquired a lawyer to fight my case and finally did get the money minus what I had to pay the lawyer. The other policy, which would have paid the balance of the mortgage to my house, had to be used to pay bills. It is so ironic that we had taken a second mortgage on the business and did not get mortgage insurance, as we had on the first mortgage.

My goal was to keep Bronner's Lounge open until I could find a buyer. I did not need to be convinced to get out of this business. With six daughters and four of them still in school, it was too much to handle. My biggest regret about selling the business was that I was too proud to ask my family for advice. I made some huge mistakes. I did not get a lawyer to represent my interest and relied on an accountant I trusted and the real estate agent who had sold us the property in the first place. It was the weirdest thing ever. The sale price was probably low, and I did not know the first thing about negotiating a fair price.

The business had been robbed a total of five times after we purchased it and I do not know how many times it was robbed before but had heard that it was more than five. The real problem for me was, I had never sold any property. I trusted the real estate agent as he seemed like an honest man, and he had also recommended the accountant that we used. My common sense told me to get a lawyer to represent me, but I ignored it because I was afraid of not being able to pay a lawyer. The real estate agent assured me I did not need a lawyer.

Who would think that he would take advantage of a widow with six children? The business was in such a mess and I owed everybody. Everything had gotten out of control and I had stopped keeping records. I was a total wreck and trusted two people that I thought would have my best interest at heart. I could not have been more mistaken. The real estate agent and the accountant had put their heads together and decided to rip me off royally. The agent convinced me that the buycr and I could use the same lawyer. That should have made me suspicious, but my mind was not working, and I was in a fog. If I had told anyone of my family or close friends about what was going on, I would not have made this whopper of a mistake. My pride would not let me confide in anyone and I paid the price.

I was so ignorant I did not know how to negotiate the selling price. The real estate agent told me that the selling price was sixty-eight thousand dollars. I do not know who made up the price. The result was a total rip off for me. He also said I would be paid in cash, but I did not know he meant literally. I was in another world at the settlement. I went alone and did not ask anyone to go with me. I was very afraid and did not know what questions to ask when I did not understand what was said. At the end I was horrified when the realtor took me into another room and showed me this small round table covered with cash; mostly one hundred-dollar bills. He said, "This is your money." At that moment I felt as though I was in the 'Twilight Zone'.

I was visibly shaken and could not count the money. He saw my expression and volunteered to help me count the money. It turned out to be six thousand dollars and some change. I was upset because I expected more money and in the form of a check. I asked him, "Where is the rest of the money?" The settlement paper clearly stated the sale price of the business was sixty-eight thousand dollars.

The check that was written to the former owners, James J. Morris and Mary T. Morris, was over eleven thousand dollars. I don't remember the amount that had to go to the loan company for the business portion. I know that we had recently re-financed but didn't know what the balance was. Another strange thing happened also after we finished counting the money; he politely said, "I am taking a hundred dollars," and did so matter of fact without explaining what for. I assumed it was for himself or the lawyer that I was sharing. I had signed a lot of papers that I did not read, all the papers were pushed in front of me very fast and I was told to sign them, and I did.

When I asked him, "Where is the rest of my money?" He answered that the rest of the money had to be held in escrow by the accountant to pay the taxes, which was a lie. I had not seen any tax bills since the business had recently been temporarily shut down until we paid all back taxes.

The temporary shutdown was untimely to say the least. Charles had volunteered himself into a rehab facility on Ogontz Avenue. I was at home when the call came from the barmaid stating that the IRS had come to collect money for back taxes owed. They took the money from the cash register and told the barmaid to shut down the bar. She was in panic mode when she called my house and told me what happened. My stress level was through the roof as I was already stressed out from the current circumstances. I told her to close the bar and I would contact her as soon as possible. I rushed to get to the rehab to tell my husband, but he didn't seem too surprised. He told me he would get the money and I would need to take it directly to the IRS office.

Our number two daughter, Kala came to the rescue. After high school Kala had started working at Health Education & Welfare on Market Street, and she was saving money to buy her first car. She was almost ready to make the purchase when her father asked her to loan him the money, and she obliged. Kala gave me all her money and I took it to the IRS office and satisfied the debt, so the bar was reopened that same day. I learned from this that if you cannot afford to give a person a gift, don't loan money because you may never get it back. In this case Kala never got her money back, nor did she ask for it, but she managed to save and buy her car.

We had two separate mortgages; one for the building, that had to be paid to the Morris Family, and one to the mortgage company that owned the business. I did not ask for help, and pride kept me from telling anyone what happened at that settlement. I thought I was going to die that day, full of anger, disappointment and stress. I was not aware of what amount was being held in escrow, but my intuition led me to believe it had to be a lot more. Still trying to trust the two of them I figured they would give me the money being held when it was proven that no tax money was due.

I was alone and carrying six thousand dollars in cash. It was so much less than what I expected, yet who carries that amount in cash? My emotions were off the charts, my heart was beating out of control and I was completely stressed.

The couple that sold us the property was given a check for eleven thousand dollars, which they say was owed to them. I could not be sure what was owed to them because I had stopped keeping records. They looked very happy and I was a wreck.

After about a year I called the accountant and told him I needed four hundred dollars to repair the steps in front of my house. He sent me a check for that amount without any explanation. Much later I asked a lawyer friend to write him a letter about the balance of money owed to me. He sent another check in the amount of two thousand dollars with no explanation of what he did with the rest of the money or how much was paid for anything. I never received a final accounting of what happened to the money in escrow; it was being held in his account collecting interest.

I never received any bills from the IRS after we had been shut down and settled with them. There was no final statement showing what he did with the money and I have no idea how much he kept for himself. I have always fought back when I was mistreated or taken advantage of. I cannot explain what happened except that I had no fight left in me. So, I dropped the matter and moved on, until the thoughts surfaced again in 2016. I have had this in my spirit for 37 years and never realized until now that it was buried deep and I am still trying to forgive those people for taking advantage of me.

CHAPTER SEVEN

Starting Over

God is so awesome and always supplies our needs. After selling the bar business I had no idea what I was going to do, but knew I had to work to survive. I was in deep credit card debt and my credit was bad. I could not get any credit from anyone until I repaired my record. All our accounts had both our names on them. It took seven years to repair and get credit again.

I was still employed by the World Book Encyclopedia Company, but I wanted a stable job and a paycheck every week. I was not the best salesperson and did not make enough money selling books. Getting no salary and only making commission on the books I sold was not bringing in enough money. God always provides our needs. One day I received a call from Mrs. Naomi Jones, who was at that time a Division Manager of the World Book Company, asking me if I would be interested in becoming the Secretary at Mt. Pisgah A.M.E. Church, located at 41st and Spring Garden Streets in West Philadelphia. Naomi was a Trustee and held other official positions in the church.

I was very excited about the possibility of working in a church office as I enjoyed my experience working with the Civil Service Commission before marriage. Going from a bar to a church office was like going from hell to heaven. Although I could have made more money working in a government establishment, I knew that I would not get the support I needed under my circumstances. My children needed all the attention I could possibly give them, and I wanted the best for them, so I made the sacrifice to have less money and more time for my family. It was a wise decision. I remembered the statement that Nathaniel H. Bronner Sr.

said, "No amount of success can compensate for failure at home."

The interview was set up and I met Rev. James L. Dandridge for the first time in Mt. Pisgah's Church Office. Our interview was very casual, and I felt very comfortable talking and answering all his questions. I told him that my skills were a little rusty and I might need help to get acclimated but felt sure that I could do the job. Rev. Dandridge was very kind and agreed that I could have the job on a two-week trial basis. The office equipment was antiquated but I knew how to use it. He assured me that I would get the help needed. I started as a part-timer in January 1979. Rev. Dandridge had a quiet spirit, very well dressed in matching everything; suit, shirt, tie and shoes.

I had an outstanding relationship with his beautiful wife, Mrs. Octavia Dandridge, that extended to my visiting them in their home. My working relationship with Rev. Dandridge lasted for fifteen years until he retired. They were like family to me and very supportive of whatever was happening in my family. Rev. Dandridge married my twin daughter, Linda Ford, and buried Tyrone Appling, the husband of my oldest daughter Deborah. After he retired they moved from the church parsonage to their home near the airport. Octavia's sister, Gloria Wilson lived with them and I enjoyed many meals and visits with the three of them.

I had a wonderful, friendship and working relationship with my co-workers. One of my friends was Mrs. Florence Smith, who also held the position of Treasurer. She worked with me and filled in for me whenever I was sick or needed to be off for an emergency or family matter. She is still a great friend. Mr. & Mrs. Keyveat Postell, Mrs. Ruth Maddox, Ms. Pauline Andrews, Tisha Arrington, Rev. Phyllis Harris and many others, too numerous to mention, were supportive. Having to raise my children without my husband was no easy task. Whenever I had a crisis of any kind in my family I could always count on support from my boss, Rev. Dandridge and the church family at Mt. Pisgah, in addition to my own church family at Nazarene Baptist. I had friendly relationships with many of the members at Mt. Pisgah that lasted the entire 20 years that I worked there, continuing to this present time.

Another New Start

After Rev. Dandridge retired the Rev. Dr. Mickarl Thomas became the pastor. Rev. Thomas had a lovely wife, Ann and she and I connected and felt as if we knew each other the first time we met. It was not so easy with him. He was impatient and made rapid changes which I had to adjust to in a hurry. The office equipment was updated almost immediately with a new computer and printing machine which was challenging.

One of the members who was a friend came into the office daily to teach me how to use the computer. Her name was Mrs. Patricia Greene. I will always be appreciative of her patience and kindness in showing me how to do the Church Bulletin on the computer. Rev. Thomas allowed me to take some classes at Temple Community College which was a tremendous help. I could learn how to do the work but was often criticized for incorrect punctuation. Rev. Thomas was very strict about everything being done correctly and would proofread everything before it was released for printing.

We had some rough times but before long he became very supportive and gave me an increase in my salary. He also married my third oldest daughter, Dr. Tauheedah Bronner and helped me to arrange the funeral service for my stepmother, Mrs. Julia Howard-Morris. He allowed me to write and print the Funeral Programs in my office. My co-worker Mrs. Florence Smith cooked some food for the repast.

I was involved in four Annual Conferences at Mt. Pisgah the last one before I retired, under Rev. Thomas. After five years working with him he was very gracious in seeing that I received some retirement money and gave me a huge retirement celebration. I was escorted from my home in a stretch limousine to the church. The whole church turned out in support. Many of my family and friends from everywhere came to support me. It was a grand affair. The Tribune Newspaper printed almost a full page with pictures of me, Rev. and Mrs. Thomas, family and friends in the Friday, October 22, 1999 issue.

Under the leadership of the Reverend Dr. Mickarl D. Thomas Sr. many improvements and renovations were made during his administration such as the installation of a new organ, a sound system, a tape ministry, an entrance to the church was made accessible for the handicapped and the white-wooden pews were padded. Beautiful new choir robes were purchased for the four dynamic choirs that combine every fifth Sunday and on special occasions to form the renowned Mass Choir. This group also spearheaded the effort to purchase the white Schaffer grand piano that so elegantly graces the sanctuary. A Bible Study was held every Wednesday at noon with lunch served for $3.00, which included a drink and dessert. That tradition is still being carried on under the current leadership.

(Some excerpts from the Mt. Pisgah A.M.E. Church history courtesy of the Historical Committee, October 1998)

"Mt. Pisgah African Methodist Episcopal Church has a long history that dates to 1833 and is associated with Richard Allen and the Bethel Corporation. The African Methodist Episcopal

Mount Pisgah Church was incorporated in April 1847, located first in the home of Richard Berry at 4100 Ludlow Street after which a lot was purchased and a frame structure was erected on Locust Street near 40th. During the administration of the Reverend E.K. Nichols Sr., the church sought new quarters in the early summer of 1942 marched to the present location, 41st & Spring Garden Streets.

"In January 1943 a fire destroyed the church foundation. This new building was almost destroyed by fire. They did not lose hope or sight of God and worshipped the Lord in Tents. When Rev. Emmer H. Booker was assigned to the church in 1943, his dynamic faith, strength in God, and vision stirred the membership to believe that "NOTHING IS IMPOSSIBLE WITH GOD." By August 1944 the church with "stars in its ceiling" was completely furnished and ready for worship and the serving of God and community.

"Over the years, many were licensed to preach at Mount Pisgah and have rendered outstanding service to the Philadelphia community and the wider society. Such leaders as Rev. George T. Sims who was appointed May 1962 and served ten years. Under his leadership the Class Leaders System was revitalized; the church entertained the 149 Session of the Philadelphia Conference; a lighted marble altar was installed, and new parsonage was purchased.

"Under the wise counsel and direction of Reverend James L. Dandridge, the Greater Works Ministry, an inspiration of Rev. Cleo Gaston, fed and ministered to the homeless. For several summers, members of this group took food, clothing, medical and educational supplies to Jamaica, spending several weeks there teaching and administering to the people. The Lay Organization provided tutoring services and a summer reading program. A parking lot was added, the parsonage renovated, and the mortgage retired."

One might remember Mount Pisgah from its weekly appearances on national TV. The front of the church was used to depict the fictional First Community Church of Philadelphia in the opening credits of 'Amen'. Amen was in syndication as a situational comedy starring Sherman Hemsley as Deacon Earnest Frye for several years. It was an honor to be a part of getting Mt. Pisgah involved in such an endeavor being shown on TV every week.

Letter from Ed Weinberger

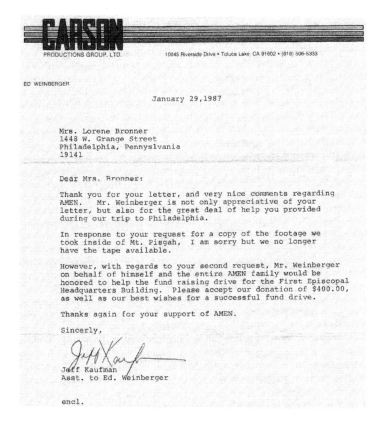

I will never forget the day the call came into the office from the producer of the show. I was alone in the office as Rev. Dandridge had gone home for the day. I was so excited to take the information and pass it on to him. The whole church was excited as the details were worked out and plans were made. I had been involved in the arrangements but when it came to the main event and Sherman Helmsley came to the church to tape his part I was not there.

My two grandsons, Anthony and Christopher, had been visiting from Atlanta and it was time for me to take them back home for school. My tickets were purchased I felt I had no choice. I was extremely disappointed that I could not meet Sherman Hemsley in person.

I did get to meet the Executive Producer of Amen, Mr. Ed. Weinberger, when he came to look at the church the day before the filming took place. I gave him the grand tour and he was pleased with what he saw.

My Home Church

I have been a member of The Nazarene Baptist Church of Nicetown, in Philadelphia, for almost fifty years. Nazarene has existed for 120 years under the leadership of six pastors. The first one was Rev. George Russell, who held weekly prayer meetings at his home located at 3952 N. Nice Street and the location became known as the First Colonial Baptist Church of Nicetown. As the congregation grew it was necessary to purchase two additional houses at 4036-4038 North Nice Street. These houses were razed to become the First Colonial Baptist Mission of Nicetown. On April 9, 1896, the Nazarene Baptist Church of Nicetown became officially recognized by the Commonwealth of Pennsylvania with Rev. George Russell as its first pastor. After serving for eighteen years, Rev. Russell resigned in January of 1914.

A call was extended to Rev. Bartram Coleman in 1914. Because of the continued growth, another site was purchased at the corner of Nice and Lycoming Streets and developed as a new church. The new church was dedicated in 1917. Rev. Coleman's leadership continued until the Lord called him home on August 12, 1919.

Nazarene was viewed as a beacon in the Nicetown community having been the first minority congregation to build its edifice. A call was extended and accepted by Rev. George L. Davis. Under his leadership, the church expanded its real estate holdings in 1936 by purchasing a 92-acre farm in Lahaska, Bucks County Pennsylvania, with the original intention of using it for an 'Old Folks Home'. Music was vital to Nazarene's ministry and a new pipe organ was installed in 1928. Throughout Rev. Davis' pastorate, he was mindful of the importance of praising the Lord in song and encouraged the development of musical talents. The Lord called him home on July 26, 1954 after thirty- three years of service to Nazarene.

In 1956, the Rev. William L. Banks was called to lead Nazarene. Rev. Banks was highly educated, spirit filled and Bible believing teacher and Bible scholar. Under his leadership, there were enhanced musical ministries and evangelical outreach. This outreach included missionaries in African, Japan, and the United States as well as street meetings, nursing home ministries, and a weekly radio program. The church's building fund was established, a bus was purchased to assist with the need for church transportation, and land on adjoining Nice Street was purchased with 3971 and 3975 Germantown Avenue for church expansion. After thirteen years of faithful innovative service, Rev. Banks resigned to accept a teaching position at the Moody Bible Institute.

On June 6, 1971, Rev. James L. Cherry Sr. accepted the call to become Nazarene's Pastor. I started attending Nazarene before Rev. Cherry accepted the call and when he became the

Pastor I joined the church. Under his leadership, the church liquidated mortgages, increased camping activities and started participation in athletic activities. Pastor Cherry resigned to accept the call to pastor the Aenon Baptist Church in New York.

My husband started our business in 1971. I went to Nazarene regularly and took all my children. They all became members at Nazarene and benefited from going to summer camp in Lahaska, PA. My children also received support from the Luck family; William and Bernice Luck. Sister Luck took my children to Bible Study, which was a tremendous help to me. Rev. Cherry and Mrs. Cherry came to my home and married my oldest daughter, Deborah. They came during my time of bereavement. I joined the Senior Choir under his leadership as well.

In May of 1984, God blessed Nazarene with its sixth pastor, Rev. Keith M. Williams Sr. He came with a vision to build a new edifice at the corner of Germantown Avenue and Lycoming Streets. The timing was right, and many members were in accord. A building fund kick-off banquet was held on April 25, 1990. On May 25, 1996 I was blessed to march into the new edifice with the Senior Choir and sing. One of the first business decisions in the new church was to elect three females to the Board of Trustees: Juanita Ogburn, Zella Michael and Cynthia Malachi White. Because of that decision, my second oldest daughter, Kala Bronner-Harrell, served as a trustee for eleven years. After moving to Delaware, it became too difficult to do the job, so she resigned in 2017.

Many ministries have been developed under the leadership of Pastor Williams. To name a few: Teacher Training; Men's Discipleship, Women's Bible Class, Pastor's Bible Classes, Old Testament Bible Class, Recovery from Losses of Life

Class, Christian Etiquette for Teens (now Teen Shop), Widow and Widowers Fellowship, College Outreach and Spiritual Brothers and Sisters Ministries. The Missions and Evangelism Departments were expanded to include the Life Threads Clothing and Sheepfold Ministries. Under the Department of Public Worship, Praise Dancers and Mime Ministry and a Mass Choir were organized.

In 1996, the Nazarene Community Development Corporation was organized with James E. Rhone as President. (James Rhone and his wife Nan traveled with my group to the Cottonwood Hot Spring in Alabama). The old church building has been demolished and a new parking lot has been added. Nazarene has always supported missionaries; currently it is supporting 24 with 16 being home-based and eight foreign-based.

On May 26, 2017 Imani Gardner and Natalie Ogburn, two young women of Nazarene, traveled to Senegal, W. Africa along with their team leader Liz Durben, to visit and encourage Joelle Durben (her daughter). Joelle is a teacher of missionary children at Bourofaye Christian School. They served in many different capacities.

My family and I have benefited greatly from Pastor Williams' teachings, seminars, community outreach programs and outings held at Camp Nazarene. I have personally been inspired to read the Bible from Genesis to Revelation three times. Pastor Williams is a great family man who leads by example. He attends his flock like a shepherd, visiting the sick wherever you are. Our First Lady, Sister Connie, and their three children have served in the church in different capacities. Sister Connie established a prayer ministry for the sick and a Girlfriends Prayer Breakfast on the second Saturday of the month. People from many other churches attend and it is an awesome experience.

Pastor Williams has a strong support system of Associate Ministers: Rev. William Dunn Jr., Rev. Andrew Jackson, Rev. Jerry Martin, Rev. Leroy McCrea, and Rev. Eugene Wright. Our services are on time and done decently and in order. I feel blessed beyond measure to be a part of two church families, Nazarene Baptist Church and Mt. Pisgah A.M.E. Church. I consider myself Baptist/African Methodist Episcopal.

The Democratic Convention

State Representative David P. Richardson Jr. kept Esther Solomon and I informed about all things political and community-related. In 1984 David was a delegate to the Democratic Convention, which was held in San Francisco, California. Rev. Jesse Jackson was running for president. It was one of the great opportunities of my life to be able to see firsthand how the political process works and how a person is elected to run for the office of president.

Esther, her cousins Rose and Ruby from New Jersey, and myself, along with Rev. Weeks and others were privileged to fly out to California with David to the convention. At that time, W. Wilson Goode was the mayor of Philadelphia and I was able to meet him as well. We had to get special tickets from him for us to be able to attend the convention sessions.

There were other functions that did not require you to have a special ticket, like breakfast and luncheons that only required you to have an invitation. David provided us with invitations to many events where food and drink were overflowing. That was an exciting experience. I saw so many politicians and newscasters that I had only seen on television. I cannot name them all, but some stood out above the rest. I had my camera ready and made pictures of as many as possible. One of my prize pictures is David P.

Richardson Jr. and Thomas Phillip "Tip" O'Neill shaking hands and laughing. Tip O'Neill was the 47th Speaker of the United States House of Representatives, in office from January 1977 - January 1987.

(Tickets to attend the nomination events at the Convention Center in San Francisco, CA)

Other people in my brag photo album are: Harold Washington, the 51st Mayor, and first African American Mayor of Chicago; Lucien Blackwell, City Councilman in Philadelphia; Congressman William Gray; W. Wilson Goode, former Mayor of Philadelphia; Coretta Scott King, wife of Dr. Martin Luther King and others too numerous to mention. I was so proud to be there and support Rev. Jesse Jackson in his bid for president. Of course, we know that he did not win the nomination for president.

The first-ever Republican Convention was held in Philadelphia in 1856. In the year 2000, the Republican National Convention convened in Philadelphia from July 31st through August 3rd. More than 10,000 volunteers were recruited, and I was one of them. It was an exciting experience for me. I learned later that my friend Juanita

Holiday, and her band, performed at the Convention Center and Worshipful Master, Kevin Myers of King David Lodge #52 was there.

All volunteers had to attend a training session by the 'Philadelphia 2000', a non-profit, non-partisan organization that served as the official host committee for the 2000 Republican National Convention. I did not know any of the volunteers that I worked with but learned that many volunteers were Democrats like me. A gigantic tent was set up at Penn's Landing for the volunteers. We received t-shirts, which were color-coded to whatever group you were working with, i.e. transportation, welcome, entertainment, community service and so on. I chose to work on the welcome committee. I still have three t-shirts that are in perfect condition with the Philadelphia 2000 Republican National Convention Volunteer logo, which includes the liberty bell, American flag and the elephant. My straw hat with the same logo did not survive, but I still use my money pouch when needed. A party was given for the volunteers at Penn's Landing with lots of food and entertainment.

My most enjoyable time was when I worked at the Philadelphia International Airport greeting the Republican delegates. We welcomed them with a big smile and gave each person a famous Philadelphia soft pretzel. Big smiles were returned to us and everyone seemed surprised and happy to get the pretzel. The greatest personal benefit was the knowledge I gained about the many historical places in Philadelphia that I had not seen.

Who would have thought that in 2008 we would be celebrating having an African American as President of the United States of America? I was fortunate to work on President Obama's campaign as a volunteer. I cannot find the words to describe my gratitude for the opportunity.

It was the perfect timing for me as I had retired from my job, downsized to a lovely apartment and had the freedom to choose how I wanted to spend my time. I took advantage of every opportunity to pass out literature, talk to people on the phone, and work in one of the headquarters, which happened to be a Lutheran Church on Vernon Road, which is the same street where I lived. In contrast to when I worked for the Republican Convention there were people like the color of the rainbow. While working for the Republicans I did not meet one person of color. It was amazing and exciting to wake up with excitement in the air and greet the day with great expectations. Having been involved in many civic activities in the past, none could compare with working in the Obama Campaign.

During the same time, I had cataract surgery and was preparing for my sister Claudia's wedding, which included giving her a bridal shower. I took leave from Obama's campaign until after the wedding, on October 25, 2008. When I returned things had really heated up since it was such a short time before Election Day. The new people who had joined in were wonderful! There was a level of energy that you could feel floating in the air. People were coming from everywhere, all races and creeds, working together like family. I have never experienced anything like this before or after.

On Election Day, November 4, 2008 I was at the polls at 6:30 a.m. and was number 14 in line. When I exited the line was out the door and down the street. The Lutheran Church was buzzing with students who had arrived by buses. They passed out material in the neighborhoods and assisted anyone who needed a ride to the polls, or whatever they could do to help. It was amazing to be a part of this history. I stayed up late and watched the election returns on TV. I could not go out to celebrate with the other volunteers because I was scheduled for surgery on November 5 and could not eat or drink after 12:00 pm. When I learned that Obama had won, I had my own private celebration, praising God and giving thanks for our first black President.

Because of State Representative David P. Richardson's influence and his commitment to the political process to bring about positive change, and his influence in the process, I never miss an opportunity to work and vote when I feel strongly that the candidate is a good person and would work hard to bring about change for all the people, regardless of color.

I also became acquainted with David's Mother, Elaine Richardson and his uncles, Calvin Robinson, and Dr. Edward W. Robinson Jr. Esther and I had wonderful visits with Elaine Richardson at her home, as did my daughter Sonja. Sonja developed a relationship with Elaine also, both before and after David passed. It was a blessing for us to be associated with such a loving family. We had a strong connection also because they were members of the same church denomination, Union A.M.E. (African American Episcopal), that I would work for, for twenty years.

God places people in our lives when we need them the most. Such was the case when I first met Juanita Holiday. I was attending the Memorial Service for State Representative David P. Richardson Jr. who was also a friend and supporter of my family. She sang "I Did It My Way," at the service. I had been informed by one of the lodge brothers that we had another widow and had contacted Juanita by phone. We had a good first conversation and I expressed my condolences.

She was very receptive, friendly and easy to talk to. Juanita's voice was so beautiful, and I was wondering who this lady was. I started reading the program to find out her name.

When I saw the name Juanita Holiday, something clicked inside my brain and I asked myself if this could be the same person I talked with about her husband passing. I could not wait until the program was over to find out who this lady was. So, at the end of the program, I got in line because everyone there wanted to talk to her. I introduced myself and said, "Are you the lady I talked with on the phone recently about your husband and the King David Lodge #52?" She smiled a big Juanita smile and acknowledged she was the person. I said, wow!! You have a beautiful voice and I did not know you were famous when we talked. We both laughed at my ignorance and we became instant friends. Through the years our relationship developed into traveling buddies, family supporters, confidants, and true sisters in Christ.

The Unimaginable Happened

One summer in 1985, while visiting with my daughter Deanne in Atlanta, we went with the family to Panama City, Florida to vacation on the beach for a few days. Nathaniel Bronner Sr. and his sister, Juanita Bronner-Garmon had Condos on the beach. Deanne was working in the West End Mall at the time at Juanita's Beauty Shop. A large group of family members drove their cars to the beach from Atlanta. We followed each other so it was like a caravan. Nathaniel and Robbie had their family there also. Nathaniel treated us all to dinner at a seafood restaurant and the food was exceptional.

We were having the greatest time ever until I received a phone call from my sister Claudia. Her voice told me something terrible had happened. In a panicky voice she told me that her youngest son, Bryan had been killed in Atlanta in a car accident. She was on her way to Atlanta from Philadelphia and wanted to know if I could meet her there. I was speechless and could not find the words to comfort her, but assured her that I would meet her in Atlanta. I asked God to have mercy; whatever I was going through hers had to be ten times worse. My mind was racing, and I could not focus. Bryon was the sweetest person and he was engaged to a beautiful young lady we had come to love. She was looking forward to her being a part of our family. We left the beach the next day and went back to Atlanta.

The drive back was scary and dangerous. It was raining the whole time and we were following one of our cousins who was driving very fast. The roads were narrow, and my daughter had to keep up because she did not know the way back. I was a nervous wreck and prayed all the way back. God kept us safe and I was able to meet my sister and her husband at our cousin's house in Marietta, Georgia. Our cousin Michael and his wife, Peggy, were very supportive and helped tremendously. They were a very spiritual couple and believed in prayer. We prayed together and received comfort from one another. I do not remember the order in which things were done but we visited the hospital the first day I met with them.

Bryon's body was at Grady hospital in Atlanta. We went to identify him and arrange for him to be returned to Philadelphia for the funeral. I could not believe my eyes when I walked into the room and saw this handsome young man, my nephew, lying on the table, stone cold. My heart broke and I could feel the pain of my sister and her husband as well as my own pain. It was horrible! I stayed with my sister and brother-in-law through all they had to do and changed my schedule, so I could fly back to Philadelphia with them. Bryon's body came back on the same plane with us. It was all like a nightmare as time was spent investigating how the accident happened while we were in Atlanta.

When we arrived back in Philadelphia, I spent as much time as possible helping my sister with funeral arrangements.

I went with her and Tom to choose the casket and do the necessary things. Tommy had been behaving strangely since Bryon's death, but we had no idea the impact it had taken on his health and mental state. About the middle of the week, after we had completed the arrangements for Bryon, Tommy started to experience pain in the chest. He was coming out of the house to go to the hospital when he fell on the pavement in front of the house and died suddenly.

My daughter Linda and Claudia were with him trying to help when it happened. I had gone home after being there most of the day. Linda called me in a panic, and I could not believe my ears. I hollered out to God for help because this was too much at once. My sister was beyond comforting. I rushed to get back to her house as fast as possible and tried to console her. The pain showed on her face and her whole body as she tried to cope with the situation. She cried uncontrollably as I felt completely helpless as to know what to do or say. The decision was made to have both Bryon and his father's funeral together since it would be convenient and agreeable to do so. I managed to help with arranging for Tommy also.

The night before the funerals, as I left my sister's house, I was very tired and completely overwhelmed. When I arrived home, I got into bed and later could not get up. My children called the emergency ambulance to take me to the hospital. After examination, the doctor told me to stay in bed for one week. I was literally unable to do anything. My body pain was so great it left me unable to function.

I could not attend the funerals for my brother-in-law and my nephew. I was very disappointed and very hurt that I could not be there for my sister and her older son, Derrick. Claudia, her husband Tommy, and their sons Derrick and Bryon, have always been special in my life and we have spent many happy times together, always supporting one another.

The funeral services were held at the Mount Airy Presbyterian Church at Germantown and Mount Airy Avenues. It was very somber. To see two caskets with father and son side by side was overwhelming to many. I can only imagine because I could not attend. Shortly after that I was well enough to go and visit with my sister. She was in a fog and could not understand why this happened the way it did. She had more questions than answers and I was very little help. Claudia had lots of support from family, neighbors, co-workers church members, her pastor and his wife and many others. She was comfortless for some time but time itself would give her peace. God had a plan for her life and it would take place in the same church; the sadness that she experienced would turn into happiness. Instead of a going home celebration, she would be celebrating a new beginning.

Sonja at Bronner Brothers

After spending seven years in the Air Force, with tours including Italy, Louisiana, and Saudi Arabia during the Persian Gulf War, Sonja received numerous awards and recognitions for her services. These included the 1st and 2nd Bronze Service Star for Defense, Southwest Asia Service Medal, and the Air Force Achievement Medal for Meritorious Service. Sonja was offered a position by the second generation President and CEO of Bronner Brothers, Bernard Bronner and started working as a Northeast Manager, in 1992. I was hired by Sonja as a part-time sales representative and worked with her until she resigned. I literally had three part-time jobs at that time, with World Book, Mt. Pisgah and Bronner Brothers.

There is an article in the June/July 1992 issue of Upscale that is entitled, "Mount Pisgah AME Church $5,000 Richer." Written by Lee Bliss, it tells of a fundraiser by the Women's Day Committee who sold Upscale Subscriptions. Because of my love for the Upscale magazine and my desire to help promote it, I introduced the idea to my boss Dr. Dandridge, Pastor of Mt. Pisgah A.M.E. Church. Mrs. Naomi Jones was the Chairperson of Women's Day that year and she and her committee liked the idea. It turned out to be a success and a picture of the committee standing in front of the church was published in the article about the fundraiser. I was very proud.

Unlike her father, Sonja worked very hard and took full advantage of opportunities. During her tenure she received many awards for outstanding performance and was promoted to Northeast Regional Promotions Manager for Bronner Bros/Upscale. She recruited, hired, and trained managers, sales representatives and merchandisers within the territory of New York to Virginia. In addition, she worked at trade shows in and out of the country and conducted annual training sessions for the marketing department.

The goal of the Bronner Brothers Company was to provide as many career opportunities for African Americans as possible. The Bronner Brothers were well known in the South but not so in the North, particularly in Philadelphia. Since the Bronner's did not believe in advertising on the radio, television, or newspapers in Philadelphia, our job was a little harder. We spread the news of the products with brochures, flyers, business cards and whatever means necessary. We rented tables at different community events and sold the products and magazine subscriptions. We sold subscriptions to family and friends, strangers and whomever we could get to listen. We introduced the products to beauty shops by taking them in our cars and selling them to the beauticians also the magazine subscriptions.

I have had many wonderful, gratifying experiences while working with Sonja during her tenure at Bronner Brothers.

I watched her grow in many areas as a leader, trainer, public speaker and an outstanding negotiator. I want to share a couple of my proudest moments of experiences.

When Bernard Bronner decided to expand the BB Hair Shows to other cities, including Baltimore, it was a challenge. We were very excited. Because of the short distance we did not have to fly to get there. Sonja decided we would rent a couple of buses and stay over in a hotel in Baltimore for the Hair Show. We also rented a couple of buses for the students to attend on Monday, which was a special day for students.

Things were looking sad until those two buses rolled in with all the students and the place looked like a hair show! That was a proud moment! Whenever Sonja was working on a special project, all her sisters and their friends rallied in support. In this instance, Woody and his cousin Cassius each manned the student buses.

Another time was when Sonja was able to solicit help from Bernard to put on a Bronner Sister's Beauty and Brains Fashion Extravaganza at the Atlantic City Convention Center on December 15, 1996. This event brought our family together like no other period before. We worked hard for eight months.

Our team of investors consisted of myself and my daughters, Sonja, Deborah, Kala, Tauheedah, Deanne, and Linda. Also, on the team were my niece, Velveta Bronner-Bacon, my sister Claudia Munford-Robinson, and Brittanica Stewart who was Beauty Consultant for Bronner Brothers and our Fashion Creative Consultant. Velveta's daughters Tiffany and Whitney Bacon, and my grandson Brandon Ford, Linda's Son, were models in the show. After all the training and rehearsals, we ended up with 59 models.

This Fashion Extravaganza and Comedy Show was the biggest event I had ever been fully invested in with time, money, sweat and tears. Sonja wanted to give models, designers, and comedians from Philadelphia and vicinity an opportunity to participate in this event. The models did not have to be experienced professionals.

Brittanica had a certain style, and she trained the models that were chosen from the model calls. We held Model Calls at the Adams Mark Hotel located at City Line Avenue and Monument Road. We worked as a team, spending countless hours preparing for this event.

Our designers were: Alphonso Donnell McClendon (sportswear), Bennie Lomax (evening attire), Clarice A. Thomas (girls' clothing and accessory designs), Francis Hendy (men & women's haute couture and sportswear), Alex Rapley ("ABYDOS" Couture Loungewear), Cynthia E. Collins (Allurious beach collection), James Nelson (sportswear to evening wear), Tim Crawford (the "Mad Hatter"), and Imani (handcrafted one of a kind art wear for women and men).

The comedian line-up: Brooklyn Mike (host), Charles Walden, Tommy Too Smoov, Rudy Rush, and Jvonne Pearson. Dominic Carr, a professional vocalist, performed in our show. We were supported by the Mayor of Atlantic City, James Whelan; the Mayor of Pleasantville, Ralph Peterson Sr.; our cousin Lincoln Green who was City Councilman in Pleasantville; our cousin Lauren Green; and Rev. Dr. and Mrs. Mickarl D. Thomas Sr., Pastor of Mt. Pisgah A.M.E. Church.

The show was well attended. The Adrian Ballroom was full of people and people were standing around the walls. We hired three buses to take ticket holders to Atlantic City and one bus to take the models. The weather was perfect, and we filled the buses with no problem and were on our way to Atlantic City without a hitch. From all outward appearances our show had the look of total success, in terms of publicity, attendance, ticket sales and so on. Sonja made business contacts and built relationships that have been ongoing through the years. Her radio interview with E. Steven Collins of WDAS FM opened many eyes to Bronner Brothers Products.

We all had helped Sonja as much as possible. She was working two jobs and we had full-time jobs as well, except for Claudia who was retired. The family enjoyed having the opportunity to work together. It was more work than we envisioned but it was great to pray, eat, laugh and cry together. We had all kinds of challenges but managed to achieve every goal we had set except for making the money back that we had all invested. Our expenses were tremendous, especially the cost of the convention center. The union labor prices were outrageous. We experienced a loss of sixteen thousand dollars, but we all gained and learned from the experience. We intended to do another show the following year, but things happened beyond our control that affected all of us and caused us to scrap our plans.

Bernard was generous and reimbursed five-thousand dollars of our losses. When I sold Upscale subscriptions for an extended period (until I got tired), Bernard gave me the total amount of the sale price. He continues to be supportive of many family activities and meets us wherever we are when something special is going on. He is like a son to me and a brother to my daughters.

During the time of our show I was suffering with pain in my right hip and it was not easy for me to walk. By February 26, 1997 I was scheduled to have surgery on my right hip. My God has always supplied all my needs and when I needed surgery my Orthopedic Doctor, who had treated me when I had the broken arm, recommended Dr. Richard Rothman of the Rothman Institute. I felt very good about it and was never disappointed. Dr. Rothman did an outstanding job and I never had a complication or any regret from him during my surgery. After a few weeks of rehabilitation, I was able to go to the Bronner's Hot Spring at Cottonwood, AL and receive healing from the miracle water there. When I returned I was done with therapy.

Didn't Know the Gun...

"Didn't know the gun..." was the title of an article in the Philadelphia Daily News printed on May 2, 1998. The sub title was "Man, 21, guilty of killing his cousin 14," by Dave Racher, a Daily News Staff Writer.

On April 16, 1997 my life was turned upside down again by a sudden tragedy and a horrific incident that devastated our family. My daughter Deanne called me that morning, screaming over the telephone, "Mommy, Christopher is dead!!" I asked her, "What? What did you say?" "Christopher is dead!!" ""No, No", was all I could reply immediately.
By this time, I was sitting on the floor clutching the phone with tears running down my face. How could this be true? I asked her where she was, and she replied, "I am at the hospital." I told her I was coming, and she said, "No don't come here." She told me to come to his cousin's house, as that was where they were going in order to find out what happened. I said I would meet her there. This bright sunshiny winter day had suddenly turned into a nightmare.

Christopher Lamar Birdsong was my fifth grandson, born on November 3, 1982. His parents were Anthony Birdsong and Deanne Birdsong Hale. Christopher had an older brother, Anthony Joseph Birdsong (affectionately called Tony) who was in college at Penn State University when this awful incident happened.

I had seven grandsons at this time with one being deceased shortly after birth: the first was Christopher Tyrone Appling (deceased), Anthony Joseph Birdsong, Donald Austin, Tyrone Appling, Christopher Lamar Birdsong, Brandon DeShaun Ford, and Shaun DeAndre Ford. These grandsons have been a blessing in my life and I have been involved in their lives since birth. Who knew that in a few years I would be blessed with a granddaughter and another grandson.

NEWSPAPER ARTICLE

PAGE 10　　　　PHILADELPHIA DAILY NEWS　　　　MAY 2, 1998

Didn't know the gun...

by **Dave Racher**

Daily News Staff Writer

Ralph Mayrant, 21, said he once deliberately shot his pet dog in the leg for growling. The dog survived.

But on Feb. 16, 1997, Mayrant says he accidentally shot and killed his 14-year-old cousin while playing "cops and robbers."

Mayrant, of Glenloch Street near Bridge, told Common Pleas Judge Lisa A. Richette yesterday that he thought the gun was empty when he squeezed the trigger inside his apartment.

Assistant District Attorney Mark Gilson said Christopher Birdsong, of 65th Avenue, died after being shot in the eye "at close range."

He said Mayrant should have checked the gun.

"I know you did not mean to

Man, 21, guilty of killing his cousin, 14

kill your cousin, that is clear," said Richette.

"But your action was so reckless that it rose to the level of malice."

She then convicted Mayrant of third-degree murder and committed him to prison to await sentencing.

Richette told Mayrant that instead of pointing the gun "at a vital part of the body," he could have aimed at Birdsong's leg, "like you did with your dog. When you take a human life in this society, you have to pay a penalty."

Mayrant, who has no prior record, faces at least a mandatory five to 10 years in prison. Third-degree murder carries

a possible 20- to 40-year jail term.

When Mayrant was asked why he originally told police that Birdsong had shot himself, he replied, "I was scared. I thought of what his mom would think, and I didn't want to tell anybody because we were so close. How could I tell somebody that I just shot my own cousin?"

Defense lawyer Darryl A. Irwin argued that Mayrant "did something supremely stupid," but honestly believed that there were no bullets in the gun when he shot.

Along with the murder weapon, police found a disabled shotgun, a bow and arrow set and a bullet from an unknown weapon in the apartment.

"I think he has a morbid, intense fascination with firearms," said Richette.

"And that makes me worried about this young man." ■

Later, on the day Christopher died, we tried to put the pieces together to figure out how this terrible thing had happened. My daughter had reluctantly agreed for Christopher to go to his Cousin Ralph Mayrant's house to spend the night. One of his favorite cousins, Azerene, had come from Atlanta to visit and Christopher wanted to spend some time with her before she went back. He was very excited about going and begged her until she gave in and consented to let him go.

We did not see Ralph as the police had arrested him and taken him into custody. His cousin was there and tried to explain what happened. The copy taken from the newspaper article (previous page) sums it up well.

Christopher will always be remembered as an intelligent sweet spirit, with a playful personality. He learned quickly and had a natural talent for acting. During the summer he spent time learning the craft at the Freedom Theatre on Broad Street in Philadelphia. He attended summer camp programs at the Camp in Lahaska, PA sponsored and owned by the Nazarene Baptist Church, located at 3975 Germantown Avenue in Philadelphia, where he became a member about age ten. Mt. Pisgah Church located at 41st and Spring Garden Streets in West Philadelphia proved to be a blessing to my grandsons as well.

During the summer months when they were staying with me, I would take them to work with me and keep them until noon, so they could attend Vacation Bible School for two weeks. I had full support and cooperation from Brandon and Shaun's grandfather, whom they lovingly called (Pop Pop). His name is James Ford. I call him Mr. Ford. He is their father's father. Mr. Ford is a man who supports his family wholeheartedly with all his resources, and he helped me by picking up the children at noon from the church and bringing them whenever it was necessary.

Christopher's funeral service was held at our church, Nazarene Baptist, on April 21, 1997, officiated by our pastor, Rev. K. Marshall Williams Sr. The service was well attended by many family members, classmates and friends. My employer at that time was Rev. Dr. Mickarl D. Thomas, Pastor of Mt. Pisgah A.M.E. Church. He attended the service and spoke very kindly of Christopher as he knew him from Vacation Bible School.

Yet another unexpected traumatic experience took a tremendous toll on all our family. His mom and I sought counseling for a period afterward which helped us to accept what happened. His brother Anthony would not go to counseling despite our telling him that it would help. He and his brother were very close and loved each other unconditionally. Tony left school and it was a while before he went back and finished college. He graduated from Temple University (cum laude) a year or two later. We celebrated on a cruise to several islands in the Caribbean. It was also a blessing to find out that Deanne was expecting another child.

Why Do We Hate Each Other So Much?

Could it be that because other people hate us it makes us hate ourselves? We are supposed to love everybody regardless of Race, Creed, or Color. Since charity starts at home why don't we love each other first and then love everyone else? I have more questions than answers, but I know that I am a God-fearing woman who tries to live a Christian life and keep the Ten Commandants, one of which states that you should love your neighbor as yourself. That is hard to do when you have this inbred hatred for yourself.

Recently I had an experience at a Korean Nail Shop that was very strange. I had a manicure and pedicure done and when I was finished I went to the dry station and a black lady was already there. I sat facing her and neither of us spoke a word, but I could feel something emanating from her like an evil spirit. I wanted to say something but could not find the words and my mind tried to start a conversation, but I couldn't. When I would look at her she was trying not to look at me and avoided eye contact. I sat there, very uncomfortable until she got up. She didn't leave but went to the front of the shop and sat in a chair for a while before she left. I assumed that her nails were not dry, but she didn't want to sit facing me any longer. I felt that an evil spirit had been in my presence.

I didn't see her leave, but she sat there for what seemed like five or ten minutes before I noticed she was gone. This feeling that I get sometimes is so weird, perhaps I am not the only black person who feels this way. What way is this way? Whenever I go to a public place which I consider 'upscale' and frequented by upscale white people, I feel special until a bunch of black people come in; then I hear myself thinking, "Where did they come from," as though I should be the only one allowed in. What is that stupid feeling? Why should being around a bunch of white people make me feel special about myself? It's really a mixed emotion that I think stems from slavery. It also stirs hatred toward whites because they are so privileged and have so many opportunities that we as black people do not have.

It's hard to love people who mistreat you. I hope to live long enough to find the answer to this amazing problem with people. Sometimes I do not like people. My Pastor, Keith Marshall Williams admonishes us to hate the sin, but love the person.

I pray for God to give me wisdom to understand things that are too great for me. One of the questions that I would like to have answered is why, from childhood, I have craved to have long straight hair. God made us all different and long straight hair was not one of my gifts. My hair has never grown below my shoulders and has always been hard to manage because it has an unusually tight curl, which makes it hard to comb. It hurts when I comb it.

I am happy to be over my 'buy hair days', when I thought that having extra hair on my head made me look beautiful. I know now that beauty comes from within and is not the sum of the amount of hair on my head. I must strive to take care of my whole self, mind, body and spirit. I must live a life that is pleasing to God and not man.

When television was invented, and we saw images of white people with long hair, did that set black women on the course of buying hair? There seem to be more commercials on hair and makeup on TV than any other. These constant visions of long hair have become entrenched in our thought processes and have us believing that we need to look like that to be beautiful. I started to change my thinking about hair when I noticed the prices were continually rising and sometimes I felt humiliated by the treatment I received when buying hair in the stores that have dominated the hair supply business. I don't need to buy hair to look like someone else.

Black people could change the whole economy of the hair industry if they would stop buying wigs and hairpieces. Think of the money you could save just by taking care of your God-given hair. Many times, when I was buying hair I have felt offended by the owners of hair stores. They would act as if they did not appreciate my buying from them, giving me a suspicious look when I enter their establishment. It took me a long time to realize that I did not need to buy extra hair. I have tried many ways and products to help manage my God-given hair and learned that the best products to use are the ones manufactured by black Hair Care Companies.

I recommend the (BB) Bronner Brothers Hair Care products because I have used their products for the whole seventy years they have been in business. I have nothing to gain financially or otherwise by telling this truth. My motivation comes from wanting to help my people grow by sharing information that would be beneficial.

Black women spend millions of dollars on false hair. God made us beautiful, unique, and smart with many different shades of color. Some of us have hair that is hard to manage. Some people lose their hair for many different reasons, and others don't want to do the work required to maintain their God-given hair, so they buy a wig. If you are going to wear a wig you should comb it and care for it just as you do your own hair. In addition, you have to care for your own hair while it is being covered by other hair. Many people have become bald from not caring for their hair while it is covered up. Some people don't want to do the work and go out looking crazy, with matted wigs on their heads, hair flowing down to their behinds which does not look pretty, in my opinion. Spending money for no good reason except to get attention perhaps? Our young black children are emulating everything they see on TV, and some of them have way too much hair on their heads, making them look too grown-up.

There are many things I am grateful for in my life but one thing that stands out above the rest is my personal relationship with God. I am so appreciative of God letting me live long enough to know who He is and to appreciate what He has done in my life. I have a peace that I did not experience in my early years of life that goes beyond understanding. I know that it comes from God and His love for me that allows me to have this peace. I do not know the proper words to express my appreciation to my Heavenly Father. I love the Lord with all my heart and enjoy this personal relationship beyond measure.

Someone asked the question, "If you had your life to live again what would you change? My answer is, "I would spend more time building a personal relationship with God the Creator of Heaven and Earth and less time chasing after my husband and material things of life.

I would have prayed more about everything before making decisions; I would have trusted God for guidance and direction through prayer and meditation. I would have listened to God's guidance and not other people. I would have worried less and trusted God more. I would have been less cocky and more humble, knowing that I could not live this life without God. I would not have let pride get in my way. I would have admitted when I was wrong and not been ashamed to ask for forgiveness. I would have sought to get more education so that I would have the skills to get higher paying jobs that would have afforded me the lifestyle that I desired. I would have put God first, family second, education and jobs in that order. Love is one of the greatest gifts in life.

John 3:16 For God so loved the world that He gave His only begotten Son, that whosoever believeth in him should not perish, but have everlasting life. (KJV)

God is love, and we should love Him first and then each other. I believe we are our brother's keeper, but we should not get it twisted and put others before God.

CHAPTER EIGHT

My Long Term, Long Distance Relationship

After my husband was murdered I thought I was going to die because I had so much fear about everything. I was diagnosed with high blood pressure and mitral valve prolapse. I hate taking medication but had to take it every day. I wanted to meet a man that would be compatible with me, secure in himself, not jealous, and God fearing. It was my intention to marry again. I believe in marriage and when two people have a great love for each other and are compatible and know how to respect each other it makes for a great relationship. Two people working together can accomplish more than one person alone.

It is hard for me to start a new relationship. I do not make friends easily and most people that I meet are introduced to me by people that I know. Such was the case when my friend, Esther Solomon, introduced me to her brother, Oliver Jones. He happened to live in Jacksonville, Florida. We had a strong attraction for one another upon meeting and eventually we started dating. Having a long-distance relationship was something new and exciting. I had the freedom I needed, yet I was committed to the relationship because I have always had one relationship at a time. It was never in my DNA to cheat. I believe in love and commitment. This relationship lasted a long time because we both had experienced extreme jealousy in our first marriages and it was a great relief to meet someone who did not exemplify those traits. I choose to trust until I am proven wrong.

These years were exciting, and we vacationed together every summer. My first cruise was taken with my friend and it was quite an experience. We both flew to Miami where we boarded the ship. I did not know whether he was in the cabin already or not. When I arrived he was not there, so I set out to look for him. We were elated to finally get together in our cabin and forgot about going up top to wave good-bye to the people. When we finally finished greeting each other and came back to earth, the ship was way out in the ocean. I looked out of the window saw the ship was moving and exclaimed, "Oh my goodness the ship is moving!" Up to that point we did not know we were cruising.

Our ports of call were: St. Thomas, St. Marten, and Nassau. We met three lovely couples that we had dinner with each night. Two of them were newlyweds. Our first cruise was the beginning of many vacation trips together.

One of the vacations we enjoyed was a week in the Pocono Mountains, in a log cabin near a lake. Bushkill Falls was a wonderful place to interact with nature and enjoy the beauty that God made. San Francisco was another memorable vacation. We cruised on the San Francisco Bay to Alcatraz Island and the infamous and notorious former federal prison.

We also traveled to other places like Panama City; St. Augustine; Dothan, AL at the Cottonwood Hot Spring; Mobile, AL; Gasport, AL (my hometown); Lake Butler, FL; New York; Atlantic City; Plainfield, NJ and many other places too numerous to mention.

After eighteen years of dating, we realized that our differences were too numerous to make for a happy marriage. Since we both believed in God and the way we were living was sinning against God, we decided to dissolve our relationship as it was and still be friends and keep in touch from time to time. We mutually agreed that it was best to go our separate ways, with no anger or blame. It was a season in my life that was very special with many good memories. Our families connected and still have a connection.

God connects us with people to help us on this journey of life. When I first met Oliver, I was a smoker of cigarettes. I knew it wasn't good for my health, but I enjoyed the way it made me feel. He was not a smoker and was annoyed whenever I smoked in his presence. Not wanting to make him uncomfortable, I would not smoke when we were together. He encouraged me to stop smoking, and common sense kicked in and made me realize that it was a bad habit that I did not have to do. Stopping for short periods was easy but stopping altogether was more difficult. It took longer than I thought without any medical help.

I started smoking when my husband and I had the bar business. It seemed most people were smoking, especially those who drank alcohol. Movie Stars were smoking when they made movies and I thought that made them special, so I wanted to emulate those people. Besides, my husband smoked cigarettes and I wanted to do what he did. My husband's advice to me was, "Don't start smoking because you will become addicted." My answer to him was, "No I will not," but of course I was wrong and really realized how wrong I was when it took me about two years to get it out of my system and stop permanently. I thank God and my friend Oliver for helping me to get rid of such a nasty habit.

Thirteen Years as Proprietor of a Rental Property

When the opportunity presented itself for me to obtain a property on the block where I had lived for 32 years, I was excited. It was located at the opposite end of the block. It was convenient and should not be a problem, I thought. My idea of investing in real estate would come to fruition.

This property was a duplex and had tenants living inside at the time I purchased it. I was able to purchase the property at what I thought was a reasonable price until I realized afterward the condition it was in and how much work was needed. The first-floor apartment was a mess from front to back. I had an eerie feeling about the paneling on the walls of the first floor, but I ignored the feeling. I also ignored the inspector's report that outlined a multitude of things that needed fixing. My ignorance turned out to be very costly. The floors were horrible. The kitchen was deplorable. The stove and sink were detestable. It did not look like anyone should be living there. My priority was to get this place clean and safe for someone to live in.

After settlement, I gave notice to the tenants on the first floor that they would have to relocate because I had to renovate the premises. I had no idea how much money I would put into this property. By the time it was ready for someone to move into the first floor I had spent about thirty thousand dollars and had a contractor who did shoddy work to boot. I was taken advantage of by a fast-talking contractor who bought too much material and kept it for himself.

Wall paneling on the walls covered up a lot of water damage and bad wiring on the first floor. The second-floor apartment was not as bad, but it also needed repairs. The first thing was to have all new electrical wiring on the first floor. The entire first floor was remodeled with new everything. I was not completely satisfied with the work, but the place looked beautiful and I would have been proud to live there myself. The next order of business was to find a tenant.

After the first floor was finished and ready for a tenant, I thought I had it made, but it was only the beginning of 13 years of repairs upstairs, downstairs and in the basement. The house had been neglected for so long it needed repairs everywhere. Everything that had been done was shoddy and as cheap as possible. What I perceived as a good deal turned out to be a nightmare. I would not be defeated. I fixed everything that needed repair in a timely manner. Every month something new would break down.

Screening renters is not an easy process. People would make appointments and not show up. You needed to charge a processing fee when a prospect would fill out the rental application. This fee would allow you to get a credit check on the individual without having to take it from your pocket. It was difficult for me to take a person's application fee if by talking to them I determined I could not rent to them. Sometimes I would mail the fee back to them with a note. It takes a stouthearted person to be a landlord. People will take advantage and not care about your property. Some tenants act as though they are doing you a favor. They also know how to get over. In my experience when I had an occasion to take a tenant to the court, the system was in favor of the tenant. It was truly amazing, and I was appalled at the way things turned out for me.

A woman and her daughter rented an apartment from me and after seeing a program on the Oprah Winfrey Show about hoarders, I would have to say they did fit into that category. The place was packed from front to back. To move about you had to walk around and through stuff. They had the use of the basement and it was also full of stuff. It was amazing that anyone could live in a place with so much stuff. It was a fire hazard and I was afraid for them. I pleaded with them for four years to remove some of their stuff and they promised me they would. From time to time I would check only to find out that some stuff had been moved from one area to another to make it look as though some things had been eliminated but it did not happen.

At one point in time the main drainpipe started to leak and was replaced promptly, but water had accumulated on the basement floor where my tenants had all kinds of stuff.

I asked them to move things to avoid damage, and they did not. The result was that I had to go to court to have them evicted. I wound up using all their deposit money to pay the rent when they stopped paying.

When they moved out they left stuff and furniture that I paid someone to remove, which was a painful and disgusting process. I took pictures of the stuff they left in the apartment to show the judge when we went to court. The judge looked at the pictures and asked the tenant, "Is this your furniture?" Her reply was "No", and the judge took her word against mine. I was so annoyed and angry when I left that courtroom. I wanted the opportunity to tell the judge what I thought about her and told myself, if I ever saw her anywhere I would let her know how unfair she was. Unfortunately, I have never seen her since.

Leaking Roof

One of the most difficult problems I had with the building was a leaking roof. I had a new roof put on the building but shortly afterward the porch part of the roof started to leak. The roofer came back a couple of times and tried to correct the problem. He did everything he knew to do but the problem would always happen after a heavy, blowing rain. The roofer determined it was the windows above the porch that were not properly installed, and the blowing rain would come in around the windows. I could not prove that he was wrong, so I hired a window contractor to install two new windows. Each time a heavy rain would come with blowing wind the roof would still leak. The new windows did not correct the problem.

I hired another contractor to look at the problem and he determined that the loose shingles in the front of the porch caused the leak. I spent about nine hundred dollars getting the shingles fixed. The leak did not go away. I hired another roofer who put a special coating on the porch roof that he was sure would correct the situation. Each time a heavy blowing rain occurred fear would grip my heart and I would wait for the dreaded news that the roof was leaking again. It always happened in the same spot in the ceiling. Sometimes if the call did not come, I would call to verify if it happened. This went on for about three years. I was at my wits end and just wanted out of this business. I consider myself a very strong person, but this problem had just about gotten the best of me.

I had a break in between leaks and got new tenants. The apartment had been refurbished for the new tenants and no heavy blowing rain had occurred for some time. I thought I had it made. Another heavy blowing rain came soon after the new tenants moved in and I knew the problem was still there. The new tenant was an ambitious young man and he knew how to build houses and fix things. He informed me that he could fix the problem. He said if I bought the material he would only charge for the labor. He told me he would tear out the ceiling from the inside and go up to the porch roof. He found the solution to the problem and fixed it. After three years of spending money on the same problem, I was relieved to get the job done right. The heavy blowing rain did not cause the leak on the porch after he fixed it. I was grateful to be relieved of worry each time a heavy blowing rain came.

The total cost of the roof problem was approximately two thousand five hundred and fifty dollars. The problems kept coming! The next two major events were installing the main drainpipe and a new heater. The craziest thing happened when I hired the Stanley Steamer Company to clean the carpet. The young man they sent out needed water for his equipment and instead of asking where he could get the water, he started turning valves on top of the heaters.

Water came pouring down from the pipes and I was astonished and very upset. I told him whatever he did to cause the problem he had better fix it. He called his employer and explained the situation. Bottom line, a plumber had to be called. The expansion tank over the heater had overflowed and caused the leak. It had to be replaced. The manager at Stanley Steamer told me to hire a plumber and they would reimburse me for the cost. I called a plumber from the yellow pages and he came out the same day and fixed the problem. I was fortunate to have a credit card to pay the plumber. To get my money back right away I had to go to Doylestown to the Stanley Steamer Company, which was an extra burden that added to the aggravation and stress that the problem caused.

Ignorance is very costly, and it cost me a lot. I did not learn anything about the taxes and licenses from the bar we had for eight years. We had an accountant who was supposed to take care of that. It didn't take me long to realize that owning anything that you make money from has a bunch of taxes and licenses attached to it. The City of Philadelphia has a Business Privilege Tax, Net Profits Tax, and a Rental License Fee that has to be paid annually. I would recommend, for anyone who has a rental property, that they join the National Tenant Network. It provides helpful information and a monthly newsletter to keep you informed of any changes in the laws. You can also hire a lawyer through the organization to represent you in an eviction case. They have meetings from time to time that all members are invited to attend. You will have the opportunity to get your questions answered and share information with other rental property owners. There is an annual fee to keep your membership in force.

When I had taken all that I could stand, I decided to sell the property. Thirteen years of fixing all the broken and worn out parts of that building was enough. It was like I had built another house inside of the old house. It reminded me of an old car I had for fifteen years. It seemed that I had replaced every part of that car and it was still breaking down. This time I walked away with a substantial amount of money unlike the bar sale. Not having that responsibility anymore meant more to me than the money. It gave me so much peace and a wonderful change in my life.

Moving from Philadelphia to Delaware

After 45 years of living in my house on Grange Avenue, and after all my daughters had bought their own homes, it was time for me to downsize. The steps had become a problem for my cartilage worn out knee. The house was too big for one person. I moved to an apartment on Vernon Road. After three years there I moved into my daughter's home in Delaware.

Moving from one state to another presents a lot of challenges and this particular day was one of them. The weather was extreme with heavy rain and strong wind, and it was chilly. The rain didn't start out heavy but as the day progressed it got heavy. Since my move to Delaware, I had been trying to get my necessary changes taken care off. One of the things I had to do was get my car registered in Delaware. My registration expired on March 31st and it was the 30th. I wanted to do it on the day before but decided to put it off. It's a good thing I waited because a lady I met in the Ladies room said that the computers had been down. I thank God I was not led to go the day before.

The Delaware Division of Motor Vehicles is in New Castle, and I lived in Newark. It sits way back from a four-lane highway and there are no signs to let you know where it is. If you don't know exactly where to turn off the highway you will miss it, which I did twice, going and coming back. When after turning around and realizing I had passed it, I became a little upset and almost went home, but I prayed to God to help me and I got a new determination to keep trying. I turned around and this time I tried harder and found the right exit to get to the building.

The rain was extremely heavy by this time and the wind was blowing. When I got out of my car my umbrella turned inside out. Lucky for me it was early, and the place wasn't crowded yet. I was told that I could get a temporary tag and registration for $10.00 after my car passed inspection.

I had to go out of the building and drive down the street to the inspection station. It was a drive-thru inspection with four lanes and an attendant at each lane. You drove in and the attendant told you where to stop and he checked your car. It was the quickest inspection I have ever experienced. I wondered about that. He gave me a paper to take back to the main building and wait again to be called. Many more people had arrived, so my wait was longer.

I was told that I had 30 days to get the title to my car from the lien holder and return it to them to replace the temporary tag they gave me. Also, the cost would be a total of $376.00, which made me angry. Delaware doesn't have a state tax, so they come up with other ways to get your money. I asked the lady if someone would put the tag on my car and she said no. So, I put the tag in the back of the car and decided to head home.

I had to stop at the bank on the way to return some bank checks I ordered. The bank put my old address on the checks instead of the new address. They didn't charge me and promised to make the correction, but it was an inconvenience among hundreds of inconveniences that come at you when you move from one state to another. Changing your address on accounts and all transactions is a pain.

A Testimony to God's Grace

Monday, July 8, 2013 started out like most days; I wake up early, pray, read scripture and do stretching exercises, before taking my shower and getting dressed. I left home at 8:35 a.m. to attend the exercise class at the Senior Center located on Rittenhouse Street near Germantown Avenue. Things were not normal, and I noticed a huge crowd of people sitting in the exercise room and all over the place. I saw my daughter's mother-in-law and asked her what was going on? She responded that the $20.00 vegetable vouchers for eligible seniors to get free vegetables were being distributed today, which happens annually in the summer. As a result, our class had to be moved to the outside patio behind the opposite building. The heat was intensive, and we did a lot of sweating.

The class was good as usual, because of a great teacher who did her best to keep us moving regardless of the circumstances. After class I sat in my car with the air conditioning on to cool off and contemplate my next move. I decided to visit my friend Willie Mae Poole at the Hillcrest Nursing Home. Willie Mae and I had many visits in her home before she was moved to Hillcrest. I called her to ask what she wanted for lunch. Her reply was almost always the same, fried chicken and cake, which was not on her menu and was a special treat for her.

My hands were full of our lunch and drinks when I arrived at the Hillcrest Center. My car keys were in my hands when I reached the front desk and signed in. I found Willie Mae still in bed. Her lunch had been served but she had not eaten. I was happy I arrived when I did because our lunch was more appetizing than what she had been served. We enjoyed our meal and talked about our experiences of singing in the Senior Choir together at Nazarene Baptist, where we met, and where our friendship began. I could tell from our conversation that her memory was failing, as she repeated herself a lot. After about an hour and a half I decided to leave and started to look for my car keys. Realizing I didn't have them I determined that they were left at the front desk, and they were. I found them by the sign -in sheet where I left them.

I had one bag and one container of soda, and my handbag when I left the front desk to go to the ladies' room before leaving. I placed the bag and soda on the table outside of the ladies' room, went inside and placed my handbag on the top of the water tank. I left the ladies room, picked up my bag and container and headed for the car. I was so grateful that I had the opportunity to visit my friend again, so I was thinking about it all the way home. When I arrived and parked the car, I reached for my handbag for the house keys and realized that the handbag was not there. This caused me to panic. I immediately started calling on the name of Jesus. I kept repeating Jesus, Jesus, Jesus. I knew my handbag had been left in the ladies' room and could have been taken by anyone, male or female, because it was all access in front of the building. I drove as fast as I could and continued to pray all the way there.

Parking the car in front of the building, I left my hazard lights blinking and ran into the building. I did not say anything to anyone, went straight to the lady's room. My handbag was on top of the water tank exactly where I left it. It did not seem to have been tampered with at all. I took it to the outside area examined it thoroughly and nothing was missing. I sat there several minutes to give thanks to God for mercy and grace.

This incident brought back memories of another time when I left my handbag. Many years ago, when my sister Claudia was living on Gorgas Lane and I was living on Grange Street in Philadelphia. Claudia, along with her granddaughter Taylor and I, were shopping in the mall in King of Prussia. One of the department stores had a big sale and we were in the shoe department trying on shoes. The whole department looked like a tornado had gone through. Shoes and boxes were all over the place and people could hardly find a place to sit. I tried on several pairs of shoes and can't remember buying any, but I did leave with a bag in my hand. We left and proceeded to other stores in the mall. After we had gone a good distance from the store, I reached for my handbag and realized I didn't have it. I shouted out, "Claudia, Claudia, I don't have my bag, O my God!" I must have left it in the store.

We hurried to get back to the store, but not being familiar with the mall, we could not be certain which way to go. I prayed for God's Holy Spirit guidance to get us back to the store. By his grace we managed to get back and I ran to the area where I remembered sitting and found my handbag squashed in the corner of the chair, I had sat in. No one had touched it, although the area was still bustling with people and in disarray with shoes and boxes everywhere. I took the time to say a quick thank you to God and thought about this scripture:

Lamentations 3:22-23 Through the Lord's mercies we are not consumed. Because His compassions fail not. (23) They are new every morning; Great is Your faithfulness. (KJV)

My friend Willie Mae passed away on August 20, 2013. I was very sad and made worse because I could not attend her going home service. I have many good memories of our relationship and friendship and the satisfaction of knowing that I did my best to comfort her in her time of need. There is no greater joy than to be able to freely give to others, unconditionally.

Surprise! Surprise!

Many unpleasant memories about Bronner's Lounge kept me paralyzed and unable to do anything to move forward for many years. I was stuck in a very bad place. When the thoughts would come I would push them into the depths of my memory and leave them. In 2016 I had an overwhelming urge to consider what happened concerning the sale of Bronner's Lounge. The sale happened on June 28, 1979 and June 7, 2016, I woke up early and my mind led me to go downtown and find the accountant and realtor. I looked up the accountant on my computer and realized that he was still operating in the same office that I had visited when we were in business. I decided to go to his office unannounced and take my chances on getting to see him. When I walked in, I recognized him immediately, although he had aged considerably. He did not appear to recognize me.

I introduced myself and explained who I was and how I became associated with him. He said he did not remember me at first. I asked him about the records he kept on Bronner's Lounge and he said that he had no records from that far back. But he did ask me some questions that made me know that his memory of the Bar was returning. He asked me, "Why did it take you so long to inquire?" I told him, "Because I was devastated and buried the memory for a while. Now that it has resurfaced I can deal with it." I expressed my disappointment that he did not send me a final statement of what happened to the money after he sent the final check? He could not remember that. I was planning to visit the real estate agent next, but I was told that he died about ten years ago.

The entire situation with the accountant and the realtor is just as unsolved as my husband's murder, and I may never know the truth about either. When I left the accountant's office I went to City Hall to look up the sale of Bronner's Lounge and there I received another shocker. I was told that they did not have a copy of the settlement paper, but I could pay for a copy of the sale agreement. The agreement of sale stated that Bronner's' Lounge, Inc. and G Q Bar Corporation had agreed on a selling price of twenty-five thousand dollars. I don't remember signing that paper, but my signature was on it.

That agreement was for the bar business, and I have no recollection of ever seeing it. I remember having the settlement papers for the building that stated the selling price of sixty-eight thousand dollars. I was totally disappointed that I could not get a copy of the settlement papers, as I had misplaced them some time ago. I keep records for years and cannot understand what I did with those papers, which I remember so clearly in my mind.

It was a hot day and my mind was reeling when I left City Hall. How could I have signed this agreement of sale and not know the amount of money I was supposed to be getting? Questions that I could not answer flooded my mind as I was walking to the parking lot to get my car. I would have gone back to the accountant's office if I had been physically able to show him the sale agreement.

The one thing I do know about settlements is the signing of many documents takes place. At the sale of Bronner's Lounge I did not know what I was signing. I never received any statement from the IRS about any taxes owed or paid to them after the business was sold. We had settled with IRS when they came and shut us down.

On June 10, 2016 I wrote a detailed letter to the accountant and sent it by certified mail. It has never been acknowledged and I have not heard from or spoken to him since.

[Copy of Agreement of Sale and Deed]

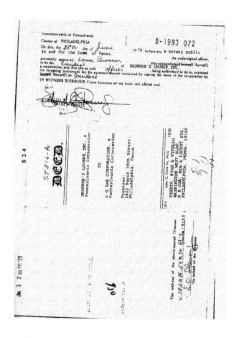

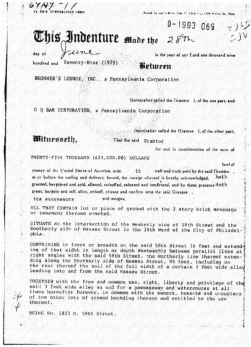

The building that once housed Bronner's Lounge for eight years and the G Q Bar Corporation for a few years is still standing. It looks like a regular residence in the neighborhood at 59th Street and Nassau Road. After the sale I never went back inside the building. I have passed it in my travels to West Philadelphia, but I try to avoid even passing it because of so many unpleasant experiences that come to the surface when looking back into the past.

This scripture came to mind as I am thinking about what happened:

1 Timothy 6:10 For the love of money is a root of all kinds of evil, for which some have strayed from the faith in their greediness and pierced themselves through with many sorrows.

My Association with King David Lodge #52

The Most Worshipful Grand Master from King David Lodge #52, Bro. Joseph B. Jefferson, was installed in October 2014. The widows were invited to the reception that followed his installation service held at the Hilton Hotel in Valley Forge, PA. We were treated with the greatest respect and had a wonderful time socializing with the group.

Bro. Jefferson completed his two-year term in 2016. The widows were sponsored by the lodge to attend the Grand Master's Ball, which was an evening honoring him, held at the Sheraton Philadelphia Downtown Hotel on October 10, 2016. Unfortunately, only three widows could attend. The huge crowd of people in attendance, the accolades, gifts and all the recognition given to Bro. Jefferson provided proof of a job well done!! In his closing speech the widows of King David Lodge #52 were revered highly and the three of us were asked to stand: Alice Baker, Lorene Bronner and Beverly Cardwell.

He talked about our group of widows and the loss we had just experienced on September 9, 2016 in the person of Juanita Holiday, known as "Philadelphia's First Lady of Jazz", and her participation in our group of widows. It was an honor to be there and be recognized among so many outstanding dignitaries from many different States in the United States of America.

The King David Lodge #52 always supported the widows in various ways; through phone calls and visits, gifts at Christmas, and a birthday card from PM John Crapper Jr. to every widow. His cards always contained a religious tract or other educational messages. Some of the Past Masters gave exceptional service as Worshipful Masters serving more than one term. James A. Williams served two terms. Past Master Thomas E. Cardwell served two terms, Past Master John Crapper Jr. served three terms and Past master Kevin Myers served five terms.

I appreciate the King David Lodge #52 and want to express how their concern and interaction helped me to get through some of the most difficult days of my life. While I am grateful to the entire group, I will name some of them who gave me inspiration and support beyond and above the rest. They are all Past Masters of King David Lodge #52: Robert Tate, James Jones, Warner Waugh, John B. Crapper Jr., Robert B. Jackson Jr., Fate Evans, Thomas E. Cardwell, Keith E. Seward, Kevin L. Myers, Cornelius Parks, Samuel Burrell, Kenneth W. Fowler, Joseph B. Jefferson, Jesse Rembert, Ernest S. Coard Jr. Anton Golden Wayne D. Crawford Sr., Nathaniel Wimbush and William Moton, Financial Secretary.

The widows have always been a priority in the hearts of the King David Lodge #52 members and have been included in many activities such as Family Day, annual picnics, bowling parties, banquets and other special events.

In 1985 the King David Lodge #52 started an annual event of taking the widows out to dinner. It began during the tenure of Past Master Nathaniel Wimbush. The event is still being carried on in 2016. The widow's dinner gave us an opportunity to meet some beautiful talented ladies. There have been as many as thirty-two widows in our group. Ethel Dudley lived to be one hundred and four years old. I used to boast about having a friend who was over one hundred. I was blessed to spend a couple of days with her before she transitioned.

The decisions to honor and include the widows, made by the King David Lodge #52, have had a positive influence on my life. Having previously been sheltered, first by my parents and then by my husband, I did not make friends easily and most of my time was spent with my immediate family. Having a large family kept me busy and not associated with many other people. Having the opportunity to meet other women who had lost their husbands kept some of the "woe is me" out and allowed me to focus on others.

The Lodge Brothers escort us from our homes to our annual dinner and back. Each brother is assigned two or more widows in their area of the city to transport. This system makes it possible for the same widows to ride together to each dinner most of the time, which makes bonding easy. Past Master Jesse Rembert was the first person that I had the privilege of riding with and Alice Baker and I met for the first time in 1985. There were approximately 20 widows at the first dinner and I was thrilled to meet them. We went around introducing ourselves and the camaraderie began.

On the way home, I thought about how wonderful it would be to keep in touch with these beautiful ladies. How can we keep in touch? A newsletter came to mind and I told Alice and asked if she would help me. Her answer was, "Yes, and we can call it the Widow's Update," all in one breath. No problem! I loved the name, but it was three years from the idea to the first publication of the newsletter. Alice and I worked hard to keep up with all the widows and inform them of all activities sponsored by the lodge that would be of interest to them.

Our newsletter started small with the first one consisting of one-page front and back. The first page was our statement of purpose, expressing our desire to stay connected and be supportive of one another. We asked for information from all the widows to share with one another. A calendar of events, a sick list, a beautiful inspirational poem and a quotation was included. The widows were asked to share information on home repairs, health issues, entertainment, recipes, family and anything that would be helpful to our group. On the back of the page was a beautiful letter from John S. Crapper Jr. who was the current Worshipful Master at that time, welcoming us and pledging the support of the Lodge Brothers.

The widows were all very supportive and the newsletter grew from one page to six or seven pages, and from typewritten on an electric typewriter to being done on the computer. With support of the widows and the lodge brothers, we have kept in touch with one another. We have had as many as 32 widows in our group when we became organized. Our names, address and phone numbers were included in our newsletter as well as birthdates and all pertinent information to keep us informed. We visited one another in sickness and in health.

We kept the newsletter going for 20 years and took a break after the newsletter in December 2009. I wanted to start writing my life story and could not see how I could do both. For the first fifteen years it was published quarterly and the last five three times a year.

Not publishing the newsletter created such a void in my life I could not believe it. Even though I had started my book, something was missing that I received so much joy from doing. During the interim, I sent out letters to the widows to inform them of anything important. In 2011, Alice and I started the newsletter again this time only three times a year. Everything was right again.

The support of the King David Lodge #52, their wives, and our widows group have been so special in my life. They have been my extended family for over thirty-eight years. I call them my brothers and sisters. Past Master Jesse Rembert escorted Alice Baker, Juanita Holiday, Rena Womack and myself to the widow's dinner many years before his demise. I have a special bond with these three ladies from the experience.

Others that I related to in a special way are: Ethel Dudley, Laura Hargrove, Alice Dixon, Mary Duckett, Mabel Finney, Norma Halliburton, Carol Hawkins, Nona Mae Hickman, Imogene Hobbs, Naomi Hughes, Cora Nelson, Gladys Norman-Bradley, Leverta Pitts, Thelma Arnold-Smith, Lillian Tunnell, Thelma Tyler, Marie Ward, Beverly Cardwell, Lena Williams, Rosie Baker-Evans, Mary Colclough, Ethel Tyson, Ruby Belvey, and Marian Burrell.

Helen Jones, the wife of Past Master James Jones (both deceased), had a special love and devotion for the widows. She and her husband supported the newsletter with frequent donations of money for stamps, and every year brought special gifts for each widow at the widow's dinners. The King David Lodge #52 was also supportive with donations of money for stamps, paper and envelopes. After the passing of Helen Jones, the wife of Joe Jefferson, whom we affectionately called "Bunny", took over bringing gifts to the dinner for all the widows.

In 2005, my friend Dora Hardy was inspired to start a Widow & Widowers Fellowship at Nazarene Baptist Church, a committee was formed, and I was invited to be a committee person. We have grown and thrived to become a vital part of the ministries at Nazarene. We have quarterly gatherings for support, comfort and encouragement to widows and widowers in our congregation. We invite members from other churches in our community to join with us on trips and programs that we have at Nazarene.

CHAPTER NINE

My Second Trip to Hawaii

When I look back over my life and consider the many vacations I have experienced, this trip was one of the best I have ever had. It was a gift from my third oldest daughter, Dr. Tauheedah, for me to celebrate my seventieth birthday. She booked all the reservations and told me to choose anyone to travel with me that I wanted because none of my children were available to take the trip, but they all supported me. I chose Juanita Holiday, "Philadelphia's First Lady of Jazz", to travel with me. From my experience of traveling with Juanita to Las Vegas, Canada, Rhode Island and other places I knew she and I would get along well and enjoy this trip.

Our trip began on May 29, 2004 at 4:00 a.m. when I had to get up and get dressed for the airport. Juanita picked me up at about 5:30 and we proceeded to pick up Daddy Street, so he could drive us to the airport about 6:45. Check-in went smoothly. We had breakfast at one of the restaurants recommended by the check-in attendant, who was overly friendly and flirting with Juanita. After a leisurely breakfast, we proceeded to our gate for boarding from Philadelphia to Atlanta. It was a nice smooth ride. We had a short wait in Atlanta before boarding for Honolulu. I called my cousin Lena Webb in Atlanta to let her know that I would be in Atlanta for the Bronner Brothers' Hair Show in August.

We boarded a huge plane in Atlanta with three seats in the aisle and two on each side of the aisle, I think it was a Boeing 747. It was a full plane with young children and babies. I had a feeling it wouldn't be the greatest flight when we got to our seats and one of the passengers had put her baby seat and baby in Juanita's seat and had the nerve to ask Juanita if she would switch seats. We both said no at the same time.

We took off almost on schedule. One child started crying and I thought he would never stop. We were surrounded by crying babies and young children whose parents kept jumping up and down trying to care for them. The person sitting directly behind me was extremely ignorant. She allowed her child to kick the back of my seat, and every time she got up she would pull herself up by grabbing the back of my seat. I finally got so tired of it that I asked the lady if she would refrain from pulling on my seat. She apologized and said she was so short that she needed to pull herself up. It did get better after the encounter. The flight was two hours from

Philadelphia to Atlanta and nine hours and thirty minutes from Atlanta to Honolulu.

We arrived in Honolulu very happy, with no time to spare before getting our bags and walking about three blocks to the Aloha Airport to board our flight to The Big Island, which was the Kona Airport. I was not a savvy traveler at that time and did not know I could have checked our bags all the way to Kona. It was an inconvenience that could have been avoided. We arrived in Kona and our bags didn't arrive with us. 'Ignorance is costly.'

We had open seating from Honolulu to Kona and the flight was about 45 minutes. It was a nice flight and no crying babies. I was not surprised when our bags did not arrive with us because we were so last-minute getting checked in. We had to file a claim for our luggage and were told that it was on the next flight, arriving about 8:00 p.m., and would be delivered to our hotel about 10:00 p.m.

The Kona Airport was small, and we walked down the steps from the back of the plane onto the ground into the baggage claim area. It was very quiet and country. We walked outside to the curb to get a taxi van. With no luggage we must have looked as strange as we felt. We were both very tired and looked like it. The taxi driver certainly looked at us strangely. Exhausted, strange looking, we were happy to be on our way to the Hotel.

When we left the Kona Airport we had to travel eighteen miles to our hotel. It was a nice highway, but on each side of it was nothing but dirt. People had written messages of various kinds in the dirt with white stones all along the road. The taxi driver was driving very slowly, and I started to wonder if he was trying to run up our bill until I realized the speed limit was 25 miles an hour. The taxi driver did not exceed it.

On the drive, I started thinking all kinds of negative thoughts like, "Where in the world are we? Where are the buildings that we should be seeing on our way? Where are the people?" It was like we were the only people on this strip of land. There were no other cars buses or anything. It was absolutely weird. Both Juanita and I were quiet on the trip. I don't know what she was thinking, but I was scared. I started to wonder if the driver was not a real taxi driver and was taking us into a wilderness to kill us. Crazy thoughts kept coming into my mind as we traveled along this desolate strip of land, including how much would we have to pay for this long ride? Our bill was $45.75, which we shared.

After seeing nothing but open space and dirt we were totally unprepared for our fabulous destination. The Hilton Waikoloa Village, a 62-acre resort. Some of the amenities were: a four-acre swimming and snorkeling lagoon, three freshwater swimming pools, a sun-drenched beach, an interactive dolphin encounter program, waterfalls, exotic gardens, trams, canal boats and more than seven million dollars in art on display. I could not believe my eyes, and we had a whole week to discover all of this beauty. There were two other hotels within walking distance of the one we stayed in.

When we stepped out of the taxi into the lobby of the Hilton, it was like stepping into a fantasyland. The lobby was breathtaking. Huge chandeliers hanging from the ceilings, huge multicolored vases and two exotic birds that said, "Hello", were some of the décor that stood out. When we approached the reservation desk we probably looked suspicious, and I am sure I was not looking so happy. I had all my necessary check-in information and when the clerk told me he did not have a room with two double beds I was livid. I told him, "We have reservations, and I am not about to move until we get what we have reservations for." His reply was, "Let me check with the manager." He went to the back and quickly returned with a room key for two double beds. I asked about complimentary offerings and was informed of the Executive Lounge, which was one floor above us, which would give us free breakfast, a noon snack, and hors-d'oeuvres from 5-7 p.m.

We walked outside the hotel lobby and down some steps to catch the tram ride to our hotel. Our hotel was the last stop on the tram ride, which made it very convenient; when we were going someplace we would get on the ride first. We had two equally enjoyable options; to catch the tram ride or the boat ride. Exhaustion cannot accurately describe how I was feeling by this time. Our room was beautiful with a balcony, plenty of closet space a large bathroom and very clean. We both were happy with our room, and I chose the bed next to the balcony.

There was time for a snack before our luggage arrived, so we ordered room service. Juanita ordered ice cream and I had soup. Her ice cream was about the size of a small Dixie cup and was placed in a bowl of ice, which cost $8.50. Four dollars was the charge for room service, and the bill was over $20.00. The price for the same food would have been so much less at home, and the difference was surprising. After our luggage was delivered, we took a shower and felt very blessed to have arrived safely to such a beautiful place.

It was Sunday morning, May 30, 2004, and I woke up early and decided to go for a walk. I walked outside of the Ocean Tower where we lived and could not figure out how to get to the walking area. It was night when we arrived, and I could not tell what the outside of our hotel looked like. Being used to exercising early in the morning I got up without disturbing Juanita and was intending to walk before breakfast. I did not want to ask anyone, so I walked around the immediate area and feeling a little disappointed, returned to our room. Juanita was up, and we got dressed for breakfast in the Executive Lounge, which was on the 6th floor above us. It consisted of a huge variety of fresh fruit, freshly baked muffins, bagels, cereal, milk, coffee, tea, yogurt, coffee cake and juices. The food was delicious.

After breakfast, we took the boat ride to the Welcome Center to get our gift and find out about tours. I also discovered where to walk from our area to other parts of the resort (we were at a dead end.) We could choose to ride the boat, tram or walk. The walking area was covered, and on each side, there were exotic paintings, statues, and the most unusual things imaginable. Because the walking area was opposite the tram ride it was difficult to know where to enter, with no sign for direction. I did not tell Juanita about my earlier failed walk attempt.

Our gift was a beach bag or six postcards. We both chose the postcards and refused the presentation on time-sharing. We were directed to the American Express Tour Center to register for our tours. We chose an all-day bus tour of the Big Island, which included the Volcanoes. We also purchased tickets for a Luau. On our way, while window shopping, we spotted a shoe store with fabulous shoes and bags. I bought a beautiful beach bag that I still use today. I can't remember what Juanita bought but we enjoyed the experience of walking around and looking at everything.

Our next stop was the Spa. It was beautiful with everything from soup to nuts: exercise room, sauna, whirlpool, steam room, lockers and showers. On the outside were the tennis courts. After more walking, around we were feeling hungry and went back for our mid-day snack and drinks. After that we took time to rest and relax before dinner. We got dressed and went for dinner in the lounge.

We enjoyed fresh vegetables, cheese and crackers, coconut chicken wings, drinks and desserts. The food was excellent. Still tired from traveling, we went to bed early. It was a good first day on the Big Island.

The next morning breakfast was enjoyable as before, and we were prepared to do some serious shopping at Kings Shops, which is about 5-10-minute ride on the trolley, which we caught in the back of our hotel. The Kings Shops consisted of a selection of over 50 restaurants, shops and boutiques that covered a huge area. It was a beautiful sunshiny day with a nice breeze for walking in and out of stores. Starting at the beginning we covered almost all the shops in the area. My main concern was to find a dress to wear to the Luau. The Luau was held at the Marriott Hotel across the street from the Kings Shops. I found the perfect designer island dress at the Noa Noa, which has all one-of-a-kind island originals. It cost more than I wanted to pay, but it was worth it to me. Juanita found the perfect dress also.

We must have spent two hours or more in the Whaler's General Store, with access to souvenirs, clothing, food, drinks, and just about anything you wanted. Juanita and I bought great gifts for our family. I bought a straw hat for myself. Loaded with bags and feeling hungry, we went to the food court to eat and buy our lunch for the all-day tour scheduled for Tuesday. Our last stop was at a children's store where I found the perfect Hawaiian dress for Victoria, my only granddaughter's birthday gift. After unloading our packages, we went to the lounge. The food was not exactly what we wanted and upon leaving we heard music coming from one of the outside eating places and decided to check it out. We stayed a little while, had one drink and listened to the music, which was nice. We made a wise decision to retire early because we had to get up a 5:00 a.m. to catch our bus for the all-day tour, which began at 7:00 a.m.

Juanita woke early on Tuesday, before the wake-up call, and we started to get dressed. We always managed to be ready about the same time and we went outside to catch the tram or the boat, whichever came first to take us to the main lobby where our bus was waiting outside.

The tram did not come until 7:00 a.m., which made us about five or ten minutes late getting to the bus. I complained to the driver that the tram did not come before 7 and how were we supposed to get to the bus on time? She was a lovely loquacious lady, and immediately replied, "You could have walked." I did not reply because I had not discovered how to walk from our area yet, and not wanting to explain it to her, I took my seat and kept quiet.

Juanita and I were not the only ones late, after waiting for two more people we were off. Our tour driver was quite a woman, she was older and very knowledgeable about Hawaii and gave us so much history we could not stand it. She talked us to sleep and woke us up again still talking. The tour lasted all day starting about 7:45 a.m. and returned about 6:00 p.m. I was overwhelmed by the beautiful and unique, magical place that I was in.

The Coffee Plant in Kona was interesting; it was a place where you could sample all kinds of coffee. I chose pineapple tea instead of coffee. Souvenirs and Macadamia nuts were plentiful. We had lunch at the Volcano House, which was on the edge of a large volcano. They said it had not been active since the 80's but there was a huge crater. The black sand beach was nice, and we walked on the black sand, which came from a volcano. We passed an area called steaming bluff, where hot steam was coming up from the ground. It was amazing to see the hot steam shooting up from the ground as though pots of water were boiling all over the place and letting out steam.

One of the most interesting places was our walk through an underground tunnel, named Thurston's Lava Tube. It developed when a volcano erupted, and the lava made a tunnel. We walked from one end to the other. It was deep in the ground, damp and dark, with water dripping from different areas in the top of it. There were puddles of water on the ground, which made it a little slippery. About halfway, I wanted to turn around and go back, but it might have been harder than continuing because we had come so far. Besides, the bus was waiting at the exit end. Juanita did not complain, and we persevered. When we finally exited the tunnel, my chest was hurting so bad; I started praying that I was not having a heart attack. I walked very slowly going forward and my chest stopped hurting. We were very happy to get back on the bus. This was one walk through that I would not repeat.

The Hawaii Volcano National Park looked like a movie scene from "Star Wars", where we saw crater after crater and black lava everywhere. All the volcanoes in this area had been inactive for years but sulfur gases were coming up from the ground all over the place. We did not get off the bus in this area. One of the nicest places we visited was the Candy Factory in Hilo. It was a family-owned business and clean as a whistle. The area where the employees made the candy was glass enclosed but you could see the whole process. Everything was being done by hand. The workers were on an assembly line dipping candy into chocolate, etc. It was not your typical assembly line where belts were moving but each person was doing a job; the Macadamia nuts, ice cream, cookies were irresistible.

Rainbow Falls was a beautiful waterfall, where we could buy more souvenirs and macadamia nuts. Our tour guide pointed out many waterfalls along the highway, which was mostly winding roads like Lincoln Drive in Philadelphia. The high hills full of vegetation also reminded us of the drive to the Pocono Mountains in Pennsylvania. Our tour guide was great! She told us many interesting things about the Big Island that I cannot remember. Our day was well spent, and we enjoyed it to the uttermost. We were glad to be back, exhausted and hungry, so we took a shower and headed to the lounge to eat. Afterward, it was early to bed to prepare for another great day!!

After breakfast on Wednesday, Juanita and I decided to hang out at our private pool for adults only on the side of the hotel. The rain came and drove us back inside. I wasn't interested in getting my hair wet because later at 5:30 p.m. was the Luau. We chilled in our room until time to get dressed. My Hawaiian dress needed to be pressed, which was no problem as our room was equipped with iron and ironing board. I wore a flower in my hair, which matched my dress. We both were looking good and attracted attention on our way and when we arrived.

The Luau was held at the Marriott, a short distance from the Hilton. We had valet service to and from the Hilton. I was expecting the kind of Luau that I had seen in the movies and was a little disappointed. When we arrived, we were given Leis to put around our necks for our picture to be taken. I thought the Lei was to keep, but after the picture was taken they took it back. They also had a flowered headdress but not wanting to mess up my flower I didn't accept it. Our pictures came out beautifully, and Juanita paid for both pictures. They were $25.00 dollars each.

At the end of the picture taking line we entered the grounds opposite the Marriott where there were round tables that seated ten people on a first come first served basis. We managed to get a table near the entertainment and where the pig was being cooked underground. We were also fortunate to get with a lively, friendly, fun group of people that included one black couple from Detroit, and three white couples from Seattle, Ohio and Texas. The food was buffet style; all you could drink and eat. They had tropical drinks as well as regular drinks including beer. No matter what is offered where, some people have to drink beer. The pig was uncovered and taken out of the ground with fanfare and picture taking galore!! The process was methodical. It was covered with various layers of leaves and dirt. The man explained that this pig would not have an apple in its mouth like in the movies. Juanita was up close during the unveiling and took lots of pictures.

Our main menu was roasted pig, Mahi Mahi fish, beef, rice, tossed salad, baked sweet potato with coconut, mixed vegetables, potato salad, rolls and something called pou that was purple in color and looked like pudding. Some people said the pou was nasty, but I could not tell because I mistakenly put my fish on top and it tasted good. Pork and beef have not been a part of my diet for many years, but the fish was excellent. My choice of drink was white wine. The desserts were too numerous to name them all. The show started shortly after dinner; the ladies were beautiful, and the men were handsome and gorgeous. I will never understand how they sway their hips so effortlessly. The dancing and singing were exceptional. One of the guys from our table was asked to come on stage to dance and he obliged. It was funny watching the people who were invited on stage trying to do the Hulu dance, some were not bad, and others were hilarious!

The show was exciting and fun to watch. When all the festivities were done, we decided to hang out at the Marriott Bar Lounge where live music and a lively group were dancing and having a great time. When I finished my third glass of wine I knew I had enough and was sure I had one too many when we got back to the Hilton and my gift of a beautiful picture from Juanita was missing. What happened to my picture remains a mystery and it bothered me for a long time that I was careless and lost it sometime during the evening. I called the Marriott's lost and found to inquire if my picture had been turned in but no luck. It was gone forever. The only negative to what would have been a perfect day!!

The next day, Thursday, Juanita wanted to go back to the Kings Shops. I was determined not to buy anything else. I could not stick to it because I saw a beautiful straw bag that I had to have. Juanita bought a Hawaiian outfit to wear at her friend Mentha's annual Hawaiian Luau at her home. She also bought more souvenirs. I wanted a cover-up for my new bathing suit and bought the wrong color and had to return it on Friday. We had lunch at the food court before leaving.

When we returned we decided to walk back to our hotel instead of riding the boat or tram. This gave us an opportunity to explore a lot more territory and really enjoy the beauty everywhere. All along the walkway were unique works of art; statures, paintings, furniture, blankets hanging on the walls various artifacts made from bird feathers, of unbelievable colors. We made pictures and oohed and awed all the way back to our hotel. It was like a history lesson on Hawaiian Culture. The end of a perfect day!

I woke up early on Friday and got dressed to meet some other ladies at the spa for a morning walk. I arrived before anyone, including the instructor. I waited for them and it turned out to be six people in the group. The young lady I had met the day before, who was supposed to meet us, did not show up.

We did a 45-minute walk in areas I had not seen the whole time being there. It was a fast-paced walk, but I managed to not fall too far behind and kept up most of the time. The walk started at 8 a.m., and our instructor was Jessica, an older lady with a fabulous body and no fat showing anywhere.

I had to rush back to my room, take a quick shower, get dressed and get to the lounge before 10:00 a.m. for breakfast. I told Juanita to go ahead because she was up and dressed when I got back. After breakfast, we needed to go back to the King Shops for me to make an exchange and for Juanita to get something for her granddaughter. Juanita also bought a bunch of Leis for the Luau scheduled at Mentha's house. When we finished shopping we rushed back and got dressed in order to go to a large pool area I had discovered on my morning walk.

We caught the boat looking very cool in our new sarong wraps, with our new beach bags and we thought we were sharp!! We took lots of pictures around the pool area, which was huge, overlooking the ocean. It was uniquely made with winding pools and pools that were sliding boards, round pools in different areas and regular pools. I have never seen anything like it. There were all kinds of beach chairs, with and without covers, uniquely made. We found a great spot to relax and enjoy the sun. Neither of us was interested in getting wet, so we settled for the sun and eating the food that we had bought at the food court earlier.

After a few hours of baking in the sun, we were ready to head back. I wanted to show Juanita a beautiful statue I had seen earlier during my morning walk, and I suggested that we walk back rather than catch the boat. We started walking and saw where they had set up for the Luau that was held at the Hilton Friday nights. It was a much smaller area than at the Marriott and the beautiful statue I wanted Juanita to see was up the hill from that area. We walked up to the statue, took pictures, and saw that people had left money in the folded area of the statue. It looked like a Buddha.

We continued walking toward our hotel following the walking trail, and that was a huge mistake. The trail took us on a long route around the back of the property and into open area that had not been developed; nothing but weeds and dirt. It was about 20 minutes into the walk before I recognized anything that I had seen before. I started to panic but tried not to show it. I think Juanita was upset with me, but she stayed quiet. I don't know what she may have been thinking, but I know for sure she wasn't interested in doing a lot of walking because she did not participate in my walking exercises.

Since I had already walked that morning, my legs were aching. Having such a sweet personality, Juanita would not say anything negative. I kept saying, "We will be there soon," and all at the same time I was praying to God to help us find our way. Juanita was still quiet. When we finally got to the end of the trail, we were at the back of the main lobby where we had caught the bus for our tour. I thanked God. I think Juanita was upset with me for the first time on our trip, even though she did not say it. We were exhausted and hungry, so we changed into some presentable and went to the lounge to eat. We were rewarded with our favorite hot chicken wings, stuffed cucumbers, fresh vegetables, fresh fruits, cheeses, crackers, and all kinds of drinks. We had time to relax and shower before getting dressed to go out for the first time at night.

We did not discover the Bar and Lounge until Thursday. We had passed by many times but never went in. Our first night out was exciting, and we met an exciting couple who happened to be a black female and white male from Seattle Washington. A black female singer was the entertainer for the evening, but she could not sing as well as Juanita. We got lost in our conversation with this young couple and found out they had been married for two years and were expecting their first child. Rochelle was the wife's name, and her husband was Allen. He looked like a great athlete and she was beautiful as well. She told us about their wedding and from what she said we assumed they had to be rich. Rich or poor we enjoyed talking with them and being treated to food by them. They described their wedding in Maui where they stayed at a house on five acres of ground with forty relatives in attendance.

They wanted to know about us and I told them how I met Juanita, and that she was a famous Jazz Blues Singer who just happened to have a CD with her. Juanita signed the CD and gave it to them. They were very grateful. We talked about our families and I told them about some of my family owning a Hair Care Company (BB). They left a few minutes before we did and when we asked for our check we discovered our bill had been paid by Allen. It was the end of another perfect day!!

Saturday morning was my last opportunity to meet with the group and walk. Neither the tram ride nor the boat was available, so I had to walk to the spa, which made me about five minutes late. When I arrived the group had left, but one of the instructors took me to catch up with them. I would have nixed this walk if I had known it was not the same as the day before. This walk was called the circuit. It was fast paced, almost like running, and some of it consisted of running. We stopped certain points and did lunges and stretches and we had to go up and down steps at a fast pace. I could not keep up and had to stop and watch from time to time. Relieved and happy when it was over we went back to the spa where I quenched my thirst with cold water. I walked back to the hotel, and Juanita had already gone to breakfast. After a quick shower I caught up with her. After breakfast I started packing all my stuff. My bags were twice as heavy because of the souvenirs and extra clothes. Juanita packed her bags Friday night so while I was struggling she was relaxing and watching a movie on TV.

The lady that cleaned our room was such a sweetheart. She turned the beds each night she had access and left a fresh flower and chocolate mint on the pillow. She also gave us a card that told the story of the Invincible Pele Goddess of Volcanoes. She always made sure we had plenty of clean towels. We left her a nice tip but did not get a chance to say goodbye. After our luggage was picked up we went to a restaurant for lunch. A chicken breast sandwich cost me $10.00. The total for both our lunches was $30.00 including the tip. The food was expensive, but all our meals were included in our package, so we only bought food when we wanted too. When we went to check out our total bill was only $9.00. What a gift!! Our expenses were accrued from taxi rides and tips, which we did not mind.

When we arrived at the Kona Airport our luggage had to go through the x-ray machine. This time we checked our bags straight through to Philadelphia (you may recall on the way we checked our bags to Honolulu.) The things you see while traveling can be amazing and one incident at the Kona Airport was just that. A young couple who looked as though they were newlyweds and were thoroughly involved in constantly kissing each other. As Juanita was standing at the check-in counter, the kissing man knocked her bag over and did not even realize he had done anything. When told his luggage was too heavy, he became very upset.

When we started boarding the plane, Juanita and I noticed them going toward the front steps, so we went to the back of the plane to get away from them. Our flight to Honolulu was smooth and uneventful. Upon arrival we caught the free shuttle to the Hawaiian Airport. We were getting travel smart at the end instead of at the beginning.

On the long flight we were in two seats on the side of the middle aisle, and it made for a great ride. No crying babies this time. We slept most of the way since the movies were not interesting. Two cups of chilled white wine helped me to relax and I only had to use the toilet once coming home as opposed to five or six times on the way there. Dinner was served soon after we boarded the plane, and I enjoyed a seafood meal that Tauheedah had special ordered for us. The next voice I heard was the pilot telling us we were one hour from landing in Atlanta, and we would be served a Continental Breakfast.

The Atlanta Airport was a nightmare as usual, and there were hundreds of people who had to get in line to go through security. Juanita got into a different lane and we were separated. I was held up when they ran my bags through the security check twice. When I finally got through I did not see Juanita anywhere but felt she would be at our boarding gate when I got there, which was B-11. Nobody was there except one employee who told me our gate was changed to A-31.

As I turned to go back, I saw Juanita walking slowly toward me. I was very upset with her for the first and only time during our trip, because I blamed her for us getting separated. Despite being upset, I was happy to see her and tried not to show how I was feeling.

We never discussed the situation, so I don't know if she realized. We had to get back on the train to get to A-31 and when we got there the flight had left. Being livid and completely frustrated I told her, "I can't do any more, I am too tired, and I am going to sit down." Juanita was calm and in control. She said, "Give me your ticket and I will find out about the next flight." Juanita did not show any signs of being disconcerted. I feel sure she could tell in my voice that something was wrong with me. Whenever I am upset it shows in my face and can be detected in my voice.

Having done so much walking at 8:00 a.m. before leaving Hawaii, plus all the walking in the airport, had taken a toll on my body. I was exhausted. Juanita came back to where I was seated with our boarding passes that would take us on yet another train ride to get to E-30. By this time my legs and my entire body were hurting.

When we finally boarded, I fell asleep as soon as possible and only woke up when the pilot announced we were about to land in Philadelphia. We wondered where our luggage would be and were lucky when we arrived at baggage claim. Our luggage was right in front of the carousel. We assumed it came in on the flight we missed.

Juanita's Thank You Letter

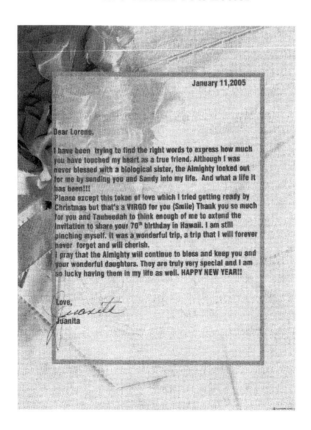

January 11, 2005

Dear Lorene,

I have been trying to find the right words to express how much you have touched my heart as a true friend. Although I was never blessed with a biological sister, the Almighty looked out for me by sending you and Sandy into my life. And what a life it has been!!!

Please except this token of love which I tried getting ready by Christmas but that's a VIRGO for you (Smile) Thank you so much for you and Tauheedah to think enough of me to extend the invitation to share your 70th birthday in Hawaii. I am still pinching myself. It was a wonderful trip, a trip that I will forever never forget and will cherish.

I pray that the Almighty will continue to bless and keep you and your wonderful daughters. They are truly very special and I am so lucky having them in my life as well. HAPPY NEW YEAR!!

Love,
Juanita

Juanita had called Daddy Street from Atlanta and told him what time to pick us up. We waited a long time for him. Since he had no cell phone we could not contact him because he had already left home. Juanita called her son and they both arrived at the airport at the same time. Juanita drove us home because Daddy Street had her car.

Soon after our trip, Juanita invited me to her house where her son Joey and wife Faye made a video of me reading my journal about our trip with pictures that Juanita had taken. Juanita presented me with a beautiful album with pictures that she had taken and a thank you letter. I thank God and all my children for an unforgettable vacation!!

The Truth About Atlanta

During one of my visits to Atlanta after my husband's death, I found out the truth. My favorite cousin, Juanita Garmon-Bronner and I were like sisters and whenever I had an opportunity to visit Atlanta I always stayed with her. On this visit, we were talking about old times and my husband Charles. I brought up the time that we left Atlanta in such a hurry and asked if she know why. I explained that my husband told me a story that I did not believe. I said to her, "If you know the truth, please tell me so I can put my mind at ease." Her reply was very shocking, but not so surprising. She said, "Charles had had an affair with a college student and she became pregnant by him. Her brother found out about it and threaten to kill him." I was shocked and asked, "Does he really have a child here in Atlanta? He told me he had a boy child here in Atlanta, but I did not believe him. Where is the child?" Juanita told me that the young lady had the child aborted so she could finish college, and her brother, enraged, wanted Charles dead. I knew it had to be serious for Charles to be rushing like the wind, packing as fast as he could. He was truly amazing.

I began to wonder, who is this person Charles. I had never seen him act afraid or intimidated by anyone. My not knowing saved our marriage. I would have left him in a heartbeat. I only had one child at that time and would not have been afraid to leave him. Charles' family protected him, and I would have never found out the truth if I had not insisted that Juanita tell me. I think if my husband had not been deceased at the time, I would never have known the truth. I had mixed emotions about it all. I felt anger, disgust, sorrow, relief and only God knows the rest. I knew in my heart that he was cheating in Atlanta and this was proof positive that I was right in my thinking. When Juanita told me, I wanted to kill him myself, but he was already dead.

The Hot springs in Cottonwood, Alabama
(Reprinted from Evers Health Center Advertising Booklet)

"Located ten miles southeast of Dothan, Alabama, in the peaceful country town of Cottonwood, known as "Sealy's Hot Salt Mineral Well," is a restorative mineral springs Health resort begun in 1927 by an oil prospector named Bob Sealy. The hot mineral waters at Cottonwood spring from a 'flowing well', deep in Alabama's Eutaw formation. The Eutaw is a geological formation known as a sand aquifer – a bed of sand saturated with pockets of water. The Eutaw is an important source of water for the state and extends from eastern Mississippi to the western edge of Georgia.

"Prospector Bob Sealy discovered Cottonwood's hot mineral salt water by accident while he was drilling for oil in the area. Upon analysis, it was discovered that the mineral content of the well was indeed very high, yet Sealy did not suspect its curative properties until he saw it heal the leg infection of an elderly man who had been kicked by a mule. Thus, the Sealy health resort was born, featuring a daily routine of baths and massages, a hotel and cottages, and a hospital unit.

"Dr. and Mrs. Ray Evers founded the Evers Health Center in 1980. Although the location is the same as Sealy's original spa, the Evers Health Center facilities were extensively modernized and expanded to include comfortable private and semi-private accommodations for up to 90 patients, an attractive dining room renowned for the freshness and quality of its food, and complete state-of-the art facilities for the diagnosis, treatment, and prevention of all chronic degenerative diseases. The center provided a relaxing, restorative environment with a mild, nearly ideal climate year-round. Patients could almost always be seen taking advantage of the jogging trails, fishing lake, and the 112-degree mineral waters that flowed from a 4,750 foot-deep well at the rate of 10,000 gallons per hour."

Nathaniel Bronner Sr., founder and President of the Bronner Brothers Hair Care Company, was always looking for ways to better his health. He believed in eating healthy, drinking healthy water and in general taking care of himself and his family. His total outlook on life and discovery lead him to the Cottonwood Hot Springs. He loved what he saw and was inspired to purchase the facility when the opportunity presented itself.

This land acquisition in Cottonwood (700 acres) has had a profound effect on my life. I have had the opportunity to go there while on vacation and while visiting with the family in Atlanta. I never turned down an opportunity to go to the Hot Spring.

My sister Claudia and I have always supported each other in everything since we were babies. When I told her of my plans to take a group of my friends to the Hot Springs in Cottonwood she was very excited and eager to go and help in whatever way she could. I decided to schedule the trip for Labor Day weekend in September 1993. There were 23 people in our group. Three of my cousins from Mobile, Birdie,

Hillard, and Annie Bell drove to Cottonwood and met us there. The others were from New Jersey, Silver Springs, MD and Philadelphia. We left from the Philadelphia International Airport.

When we arrived in Atlanta, our cousins Arthur Bronner and Juanita Bronner-Garmon met us driving the Cottonwood Vans. Claudia was the host for Van #1 driven by Arthur, and I was the host for Van #2 driven by Juanita. Negotiating the airport in Atlanta can be a daunting task if you have never been there. It is huge, and you must take a train to get to the baggage claim area. One of our guests needed a wheelchair, which separated me from the rest of the group, having to take the elevator instead of the escalator. It turned out to be a little frustrating for the people who were not familiar with the airport, but we eventually got to baggage claim, collected our bags and went outside to board the vans for Cottonwood.

It was a beautiful day and the weather was warm. The ride from Atlanta to Cottonwood turned out to be a real adventure. It was exciting to travel through the small towns that we encountered on the way. The unique town that we traveled through called Eufaula, Alabama was the high point of our trip and very significant as we would discover on our return trip.

(Reprinted from the Internet)

"Eufaula is situated high upon a bluff overlooking the beautiful 45,000-acre Lake Eufaula along the southeastern Alabama-Georgia border. Eufaula is known as the 'Big Bass Capital of the World.' Lake Eufaula features some 640 miles of shoreline and many public boat ramps and marinas. Eufaula also features the Seth Lore and Irwinton Historic District. With more than 700 historic and architecturally significant structures, the District includes Alabama's most coherent collection of intact

mid-to-late-19th century small town commercial buildings, as well as the state's most extensive collection of domestic Italianate architecture."

Riding through the town of Eufaula was an experience like no other. The beautiful homes along the main street left us breathless. We were in awe of the beauty and picture-perfect homes and manicured lawns that lined both sides of the street. We were oohing and aweing all the way through town. We had a rest stop in one of the park areas, which was clean and comfortable. As we traveled the rest of the journey I was reminded of my hometown of Gosport, where the houses were similar, of all kinds, small, large and in between. We stopped at a grape orchard and were able to pick as many grapes as we wanted for a small price. It was fun picking grapes together and getting to bond on the journey. After the grape experience, we were on our way to Cottonwood. It was not long before we arrived.

The location itself denotes calmness and serenity. It sits on a quiet road about 13 miles from the City of Dothan in a secluded area. The front of the building has a long porch with rocking chairs. A canopy extends over the walkway to the entrance. Beautiful flowers envelop the lawn, surrounded by a white picket fence. A stately replica of the statue of liberty seems to say "Welcome", standing in the mist. When you walk into the lounge area you feel at home because the decor is so cozy and warm. The furniture was beautiful and comfortable. The receptionist was very cordial and pleasant. The lounge had a beautiful piano in the corner and the art on the walls was unique. To the right was the reception desk and to the left was a beautifully decorated huge dining area.

As you walked through, on the right side of the lounge you encountered the rooms and private bathing tubs. Down the hall was the Chapel. The Chapel was serene, adorned with a stained wood podium and benches of beautiful stained wood. The rooms on each side of the building opened out into a courtyard so you could sit outside your door and catch some sunshine. In the back of the building is where you went to the pool. The hot mineral water poured from a huge pipe that came straight up from the earth and branched out with an arm on each side. Water poured out of the pipe into two closed in areas of the large pool with steps to enter and exit so that you could stand directly under the water and feel the hottest temperature, 112-degrees as it came from the earth. Signs cautioned you not to stay in the hot area more than 5 minutes at one time.

The water flowed continuously from the tubs into the large pool area and out. The water in the large pool was also hot but very comfortable. You could stay in it if you wanted, without limit. Looking out from the pool was a huge fishing pond that also had paddleboats. You could fish without restriction and catch many large fish. There were three crosses on the other side of the pool that reminded you of Jesus and the two thieves on the cross. In the early morning, I would come out to the water and pray as the sun rose over the water. Sunset was also a special time for me. Seeing the sunset behind the crosses made me feel so close to God until it gave me the sense that I could reach out and touch God from that serene place. It was a peaceful place to pray.

Upon arrival we were welcomed with open arms, and as soon as we checked in at the front desk we were able to settle into our respective rooms and get dressed for dinner. Dinner was impressive and very delicious. The beautiful dining room made dinning a wonderful relaxing, and enjoyable experience, and the food was very fresh. After dinner, some of the group went to the pool to check out the water before retiring. It was a wonderful first day of our journey.

The next morning, which was Sunday, we met in the conference room after a delicious breakfast to make plans for the day. I hosted the meeting and asked everyone to introduce him or herself and tell where they were from. I informed them that Juanita was taking some people to town later in the day. Those who were getting a massage should sign up for an appointment. After we identified the Deacon and the Trustee in our group to lead us, we all gathered in the Chapel and had a spiritual devotion which was enjoyed by all with singing, scripture reading by our Trustee Roan, from Philadelphia and Deacon Hilliard from Mobile. He prayed and led us in singing hymns. At the closing, there were hugs all around and we felt a special closeness to one another. After lunch, we took the van into Dothan with our hostess, my cousin Juanita.

Juanita has a talent like no other in making everyone feel welcome and at home in every situation. She is the hostess with the mostess. When we returned from our shopping spree, we took time to experience the water for real and spent as much time as possible in the hot mineral water. Some people who had scheduled their massage took their turns in between times in the pool. The massage therapist was excellent and made you feel so great! He worked on you until your whole body was relaxed, and if you did not sleep well before you certainly slept well afterward. The massage, coupled with the hot mineral water, was a heavenly experience.

The following day after breakfast we gathered at the pool and had a talent show. It was on a volunteer basis, but I volunteered my good friend Zella Michael, from Philadelphia, to be the mistress of ceremonies. Zella and I have sung in the choir at our church for many years, and also performed in religious productions and concerts. She is very talented and has an awesome sense of humor to keep you laughing.

Zella took the job without complaining and we were on our way to a fun impromptu production. Some people told jokes, recited poetry. My sister Claudia gave us some history about Philadelphia, and about her community in Mount Airy. Mount Airy is one area of the City of Brotherly Love that exemplifies what an integrated community looks like. It received acclaim in a newspaper article. Because the white people decided they would not move out when blacks moved into the community it has remained integrated.

Zella gave a recitation on the Prodigal Son and his journey to Babylon. Thelma Arnold-Smith recited a poem. There were people, not in our group, who introduced themselves and joined in to participate in our production. One young woman from Atlanta was excited about our group and exchanged addresses with a couple of people. She told of the wonderful time she had with us and hoped to meet us again in Cottonwood. At the end of our production we formed a chorus line and did the chorus line kicks which was hilarious. The rest of the day was relaxing and enjoyable as we spent some serious time in the water.

My cousin, Willie Bettis, made a videotape of our stay in Cottonwood which I will always treasure. He was so excited to tape all our activities. It was like he was always on the job taping mostly everything we did. When I look at the tape it brings tears to my eyes because he passed away a few years after that trip. His sister Lee Goode was with us also. Lee Goode passed away on December 16, 2017 at the age of 93.

Our activities included hanging out in the pool, shopping at a nearby mall in Dothan, fishing in the pond behind the hotel, paddle boating, playing games, walking and getting massages. One of our guests had some sores on his legs and before we left they had healed. We had such a wonderful time that we decided to make this an annual event.

Everything went super fine until we were on our way back to the airport in Atlanta. We had a delicious breakfast that morning and a group prayer before we left. When we left, we ran into a torrential rainstorm. We could hardly see, which made driving very dangerous. We had not traveled very far when one of the tires on the van hit a hole and Arthur lost control of the van and it ran off the road onto a grassy area and turned over what seemed like a couple of times.

God was truly watching over us because the accident happened after we had passed an area that had deep gullies and dense forest. What I know for sure is the van landed upright after turning over on a grassy area, which had a few trees. Everyone had on his or her seat belts, which saved us from tremendous harm.

I was in the last seat of the van and luggage was packed behind me. When the van turned over the back door flew open and luggage flew out the back except for one piece that came forward and hit me on my left arm and caused a fracture. I passed out when it hit my arm, and when I came to I could not move my arm. I did not feel the pain immediately but a little later it was horrendous. The slightest movement gave me horrific pain.

The van that Juanita was driving was behind us and she immediately acted to get us the help we needed. Fortunately, the accident happened not far from a hospital in the next town, Eufaula, Alabama (that beautiful historic town that we derived so much pleasure while riding through.) Eufaula had a small hospital and probably had not seen any action like that day, ever.

All the people in the van except one person, Zella Michael, received some kind of injury. I believe Zella's Guardian Angel gave her special protection because she was the chairperson of Women's Day Service at our Church, Nazarene Baptist, on the fourth Sunday in the same month. I was the only person that received a broken bone.

Everyone in our van was examined, given medication and instructions to see their doctor, and released, except for me. After they examined me they determined that I needed to be taken to a larger hospital in Dothan because they were not equipped to treat me there. I was taken by ambulance back to Dothan, which took about half an hour. The ride was bumpy, and every bump gave me pain. I prayed all the way there and trusted God to take care of me.

Upon arrival at the hospital I was examined in a timely manner and had a wonderful doctor who was also very good looking. He determined from the X-ray that I had a fracture of my humeral bone in my left arm and I was admitted into the hospital. I did not need to have a hard cast put on my arm but needed a sling type brace to keep my arm in place. The problem was that the hospital could not find the right brace to put my arm in, so they kept trying different kinds and each time they changed the brace the pain increased. They finally got the right brace the next day.

I stayed in the hospital for two weeks, after which time I was able to travel back to Philadelphia. I was given pain medication but had to stop taking it after a while for fear of becoming addicted. My sister had received some bruises and a neck and back strain. Claudia, Myrtle, and Edith went back to Cottonwood after they left the hospital in Eufaula.

Myrtle and Edith sustained minor injuries and were able to go back to Philadelphia the next day, but my sister stayed at Cottonwood and visited me in the hospital every day until I was released, and we could travel home together.

Robbie Bronner, the matriarch of Bronner Brothers Hair Care Co., her sister Maxine, and sister-in-law Juanita Bronner-Garmon visited me in the hospital also. Juanita took charge of the situation after the accident and was able to get most of the people back to Atlanta to catch their scheduled flight.

When I was able to make the trip home, Robbie made reservations for me to travel with Claudia and paid for our trip. She gave me a lovely gift of cosmetics on one of her visits to the hospital. Robbie kept check on us and invited us to come back to the Hot Springs to get the benefit of the healing mineral waters. My sister invited me to stay at her house until I was able to take care of myself. The doctor at the hospital ordered a hospital bed for me, and it was at the house when we got there.

I immediately started therapy with Dr. Frank Montique, owner of the Cheltenham Back Clinic and an African American. He was a wonderful, caring doctor and the treatments I received at the clinic helped me to make progress. I knew I would be just fine if I could get back to the Hot Springs and bathe in the mineral waters there.

As soon as I was able to make the trip, my sister and I took advantage of the offer that Robbie had given us to come and stay as long as we wanted to with no charge. Claudia and I went back and stayed a couple of weeks. The hot mineral water had such healing powers, and I improved so much that upon returning home I felt no need to continue therapy. When I left there, I had full use of my arm without any pain. I told my doctor I was fine and discontinued my therapy.

It was so amazing, what the mineral waters at the Hot Spring in Cottonwood can do. I experienced the healing again in 1997 after I had my right hip replaced. As soon as I was able I went to the Hot Spring and stayed about a week. All the pain and discomfort in my hip was gone when I returned home. It was like a second miracle! It was amazing to me to be able to be in such hot water that did not burn my body.

The experience was so remarkable that I cannot find the words to express what a calming effect it had on my body. I am reminded of the story in the Bible in John 5;2-4 about the pool in Bethesda and the healing that took place there. I equate the healing water at Cottonwood to the pool in Bethesda. I can truthfully testify to the power of the healing water there having been healed twice from a broken arm and hip replacement surgery.

There was a store up the road from the Hot Spring and I walked there numerous times. It was maybe 1/4 mile in distance from the Spa. One day I met an elderly white man who was very friendly and asked me if I wanted a tape of the Five Blind Boys of Alabama. I was very excited to say yes. I do not know why he chose me to give this wonderful gift too, but I really appreciated it and listened to it often. I also read some of my favorite books at the Spa. I do not know how many times I visited the Hot Spring after it opened and 2001. I am sure it was numerous times. When I learned that the facility at Cottonwood had burned to the ground, my heart felt sick. I could not digest the information because it was too painful. It felt like I could not breathe, the shock was indescribable.

Hearing the news of Cottonwood sent my mind into a tailspin and I went back in time to when I received the news of our dear and beloved Juanita Bronner-Garmon who had a heart attack at the Cottonwood Hot Spring and passed away. My only consolation from so much pain was the fact that I had so many endearing and wonderful times with Juanita at the Hot Spring. Whenever I went to Atlanta and stayed a few days we always included time for the Hot Spring. One of her girlfriends was a lover of fishing and we picked her up to go with us on one of those occasions. The fishing pond behind the spring was loaded with fish and we had a grand time. It was my first experience using a fishing rod with a reel, and her friend was trying to teach me. Up to that point in time my only knowledge of how to catch fish was with a fishing pole, hook and string. I caught about one fish to every five she caught. My arm was sore for a week afterwards, but it was great fun!

Nathaniel Bronner Sr. was passionate about the Cottonwood Hot Spring. I was fortunate to be there a couple of times when he and Robbie were there together. It was always a learning experience to talk with Nathaniel. He was an inspirational person who always shared his knowledge to help and inspire others. He saw the good in people and made you feel special in whatever you were trying to do.

I am looking forward to the day that Bernard Bronner, second generation President of Bronner Brothers Inc., will build at Cottonwood. I pray that it will happen before I leave this earth. One of my bucket list adventures is to visit Cottonwood again and experience the hot mineral healing waters that could only come from God.

An Awful Period of Car Accidents

Because God knows the future, He prepares us for each stage of our lives. We don't understand the trials and tribulations, but they are for our good. They also test our faith in God. Sometimes trials come in bunches and other times they are scattered about. During one awful period of about fifteen years I was involved in ten accidents; one very serious during which I sustained a broken arm. The other injuries were to my back and neck, from being hit in the rear of my vehicle.

None of these accidents were caused by me. and being hit in the rear always caused the same injury to the same areas of my body. I had lawyers for each accident and sued the insurance companies for pain and suffering. I had to go to therapy each time, which was one of the things I hated. As soon as I felt well enough to stop going I would stop. I can't remember a time when I was discharged from therapy.

During this period, I started to question God. "God why am I having all these accidents? What am I doing to cause this to happen to me? What are you trying to teach me?" God was silent. But deep down I felt that my faith was being tested. I believed in God with all my heart, but I was fearful.

2 Timothy 1:7 For God has not given us a spirit of fear, but of power and of love and of a sound mind.

After all the praying and questioning, God answered me through a change of heart that allowed me to declare, I will not have any more accidents. I did not for many years until ironically my car was hit from the rear. A young lady was probably talking on her cell phone and did not realize that all the cars in front of her were coming to a stop for the light. She ran right into the rear of my car as I was stopping. Neck and back injury again and therapy until I felt good enough to stop going (about two weeks). This time I had no questions. I was so thankful I was not seriously injured, and I could still drive my car. Bringing litigation against this young woman was not on my agenda and I wanted no part of that again. I just thanked God that my injury was minimal.

Trip to Italy

While Sonja was serving her tour of duty in the Air Force in Aviano, Italy, she invited my sister Claudia and I to visit her. Claudia asked her neighbor Julia to join us on the trip.

We departed from Philadelphia to Kennedy Airport in New York on July 23, 1987. We then left Kennedy for Rome, on the way to Venice where my daughter was waiting to take us to our hotel in Aviano. It was near her apartment and the Air Force Base. It was a long trip and we arrived at our hotel on July 24, at 1:10 p.m.

The hotel was very nice and outside of town in a secluded area on a hill. We had a room with a balcony facing a narrow street that did not have much traffic. It was the perfect place to stay. It was not overcrowded, and the hotel restaurant had delicious Italian food and wine. Shortly after we arrived we ate our first meal in the hotel restaurant and made plans for our early morning tour of Florence. We had to be ready to leave at 4: 00 a.m. to board the bus.

Our tour of Florence on July 26th was very exciting. We visited a huge Cathedral and a museum. We shopped at the Gucci House and bought expensive bags, after which we shopped in the open market. We were a riot trying to count our money and bargain with the merchants.

We ate at four cafes, bought lots of water, and left one bottle at the Gucci House. It was a five and one-half hour trip to Florence and back, so we had one rest stop on the way and one coming back. We were so exhausted coming back we slept most of the way.

It was a beautiful experience jumping out of the way of traffic and maneuvering through the crowded, narrow streets. Sonja had to work so she did not go with us but picked us up after the tour and took us to her nice, very clean apartment. She made a delicious meal for us and introduced us to her proprietor who was very friendly and allowed us to get some very large ripe figs from her tree in the yard. Sonja also invited her friend Max, and we had a wonderful evening.

Sleeping in late on July 26th was a welcome change of pace, and our bodies really needed the rest. Late in the day Sonja took us to visit at her girlfriend's house. We made calls home and went to dinner that night.

The food in Italy is the best in the world in my opinion. We drank wine (Vino) with every dinner meal. My first dinner meal was grilled trout, spaghetti and mixed vegetables with zucchini and peppers. It was cooked to perfection.

On July 27th we experienced the Aviano Air Force Base. Sonja took us to get stamps, exchange money and other miscellaneous tasks. Most of the stores and restaurants were closed on Monday. After returning to our hotel we wrote cards and relaxed until dinner, which was an unforgettable experience at the Spaghetti House. The spaghetti was made fresh on the premises and the menu was like looking at the ice cream menu at Ben and Jerry's. There were choices of spaghetti with just about anything you could think of. I chose spaghetti with fish, sausage and mushrooms, and Muscato Vino of course.

When we returned to our hotel, Max came, and we had a nice visit with him and decided to eat dessert with tea and coffee. It's a wonder we didn't have nightmares after eating so much food.

Sonja picked us up at 11:00 a.m. on July 28th, and we went to the Open Market in Aviano. It was comparable to our Farmers Market at home. Many of the merchants at the market did not speak English and we only knew a few words in Italian, so communicating was difficult.

My sister and I saw these beautiful green vegetables in one of the stalls and thought they were collard greens. We had seen some in a garden at someone's home and we could not get them out of our minds. We planned to cook a meal for a change and wanted to include our favorite vegetable. When we tried to buy the greens, the merchant was telling us something in Italian that we did not understand. He was shaking his head and we were insisting this was what we wanted. Finally, he picked up a packet of seeds with the picture of Cauliflower on it and we were really embarrassed and disappointed. We managed to laugh about it because it really was funny, the way we were carrying on.

Despite not having collard greens, our dinner was delicious. Sonja had picked up some shish-ka-bobs and pork chops at the meat market. Tomatoes, lettuce, peppers, cabbage and potatoes were bought at the commissary. This time we were fortunate to have homemade Vino to accompany our home cooked meal. Another good day ended with us stuffed again.

On the 29th we enjoyed a relaxing day at the hotel until it was time to leave for our trip to Germany. Max took Sonja, Julia, Claudia and I to the train station. Our first change of trains was in Venice where we had about a one-hour stay. It gave us a chance to see the gondolas for the first time. Venice is beautiful – unlike any place I had ever seen. We were excited, knowing that we would spend a day there on our return trip. A nice young Italian male sat in the train compartment with us and told us quite a lot about Italy. The trains were nice and clean, but there was no air conditioning and the air was full of mosquitoes. Unlike the trains in the States, they have compartments that seat four people comfortably. If the train is crowded, six people may fit into one compartment.

When we got on the train we had to find a compartment with seats available for the four of us. At times we had to walk a long way on the train and step over young people who were all over the place. It was chaotic because there were no conductors to tell you where to go. We had a 2 ½ -hour layover in Innsbruck, where I lost my bag with my goodies and water. The train ride from Innsbruck to Garmisch was spectacular, going high up the mountains with breathtaking scenery.

We arrived on July 30th in time for a Continental breakfast but had to wait 3 or 4 hours in the lobby to check into our rooms on the base, which were two very nice adjoining rooms with two baths. In the afternoon we caught the free shuttle bus into town for lunch at a nice expensive Italian restaurant. We went to the bank to change our money from schillings to marks. When we finished our errands, we waited for the shuttle bus at the same place we got off but realized after the bus passed us twice that we must have been at the wrong place to get the return bus. It was raining, and we were sharing one umbrella that Claudia had bought. We had to get a cab back to the hotel and Claudia argued with the cab driver about the fare. She always thought we were being cheated and she may have been right. We all bought something in town and upon returning we crashed and had a good night's rest.

After breakfast on the 31st, Sonja and I went to the Air Force Hospital to get some medicine for the mosquito bites she had gotten on the train. She was miserable and needed some relief from swelling and itching. That mission was soon accomplished, and we left for our tour, which was magnificent. The weather was rainy but the beauty and excitement more than compensated for the cold and rain. Our first stop was in Oberammergau at the Wood Shop. All the woodcarvings were from genuine wood and aged for five years. The shop had so many beautiful things it was hard to decide what to buy. We bought a couple of things and went to the Christmas shop, which was even more exciting. The beauty of the things in that shop was overwhelming.

After buying too many things to carry, we went to the Passions Theatre, where the play about the Crucifixion is performed every ten years. We had a tour of the theatre and saw the real costumes that are used in the performance. The next play scheduled would be in 1990. After we left the theatre we were off to Linderhof to see King Ludwig's Castle. This place was straight out of a fairytale book. It was a long walk to get to the castle from the bus.

The castle was huge and sat on a hill. In front of it was a pond with gold statues in the middle and with water cascading high into the air. The extravagance and expense of such a place seemed sinful for one person, King or not. There were long lines of people and it took a while to tour the inside of the castle. The furniture inside was spectacular, unique and kingly. There was a gold piano that got everyone's attention. After we went through the house, we went on a short boat ride that took us through a Grotto where live theatre performances were enacted for the Kings pleasure.

After leaving the castle, we went to Ettal and visited a Cathedral that was like none we had ever experienced. The architectural beauty was overwhelming and struck a chord inside of me that made me want to cry. Afterward we stopped and had a light lunch at a stand that had some unusual sausages that were very long and tasty. Later we went to an American Steak House for a delicious dinner. It was the end of a perfect day.

We left Garmisch a day early, on August 1st, because we had enough of the rain and cold. We started to prepare for the trip to Rome, buying food at the PX to take on the train. The plan was to eat some hot food at a restaurant before leaving. But we found out the restaurants don't serve dinner until 5:00 p.m. so, we had wasted a lot of time riding on the bus looking for a place to eat. We saw a McDonalds, but the bus driver would not let us get off the bus at stops that were not designated for the military bus to stop.

When we returned to our hotel we had to eat some of the food we bought for dinner. We left at 7:30 p.m., arrived in Innsbruck at 9:30 p.m., and arrived in Rome at 8:50 a.m. We met a nice American couple on the train, once we found where First Class was. Young people were sleeping in the aisles and we had to step over them to go to the bathroom.

It was August 2nd when we arrived in Rome. We couldn't get a room at the hotel we wanted but were able to get one within walking distance of the train station. A man at the station helped us carry our bags to the hotel. The buildings looked very old on the outside but inside the shiny floors and marble steps were beautiful.

We booked a room without any trouble that included a continental breakfast (lots of bread, horrible coffee and no orange juice). After a shower and a short rest, we took a bus tour to the Coliseum, the Roman Forum, the second oldest church in Rome, and St. Peter in Chains where we saw the statue of Moses by Michelangelo.

It was a very enjoyable tour, and it boosted our appetite and made us very tired. We walked until we unknowingly chose a very expensive restaurant. The food was delicious. Back at the hotel, we crashed for the night. Another day well spent.

We got up early on the 3rd, stopped at the train station to purchase our return tickets, changed our money at the bank and looked for a restaurant to have breakfast. It was an American Restaurant and Claudia told the waiter that she wanted bacon, eggs, fresh orange juice and American Coffee. It was our best breakfast in Rome, after deciding to skip the continental breakfast at the hotel. Today was our day to tour on our own to the Vatican City. We had learned from a couple on the train that we could take the city bus. We needed to find out what kind of money was needed for the bus and were told by a policewoman to go to the tobacco store to purchase the bus ticket. We almost gave up when it was so difficult to find the tobacco store. After finding it, we bought several items.

On the way to the store, Julia noticed a man who looked African, selling beautiful leather belts that were spread out on the sidewalk. He told her the price was 20 mil, then changed to 15 mil. Julia decided to buy a belt and Claudia wanted one also, so they offered him 25 mil for two belts. After they got the belts and started to walk away he said that they had only paid for one and he wanted 20 mil each. Claudia and Julia started to argue with him, pointing a finger in his face, while Sonja and I looked at them and cracked up laughing. It was comical to see them in action. I am so sorry I didn't have my camera ready to get that picture. The man gave up and let them have the belts.

After buying the bus tickets for 700 lire, we never used the ticket, which was puzzling. It was a 20-minute ride to the Vatican from our location. Once we went inside of St. Peters Square, it was like in another world back in time. The entire view was overwhelming. I cannot describe the feeling of seeing so much history. Once inside the Cathedral we walked around almost in a daze. We prayed in two of the Chapels. There was so much beauty I had another crying experience. The statues all around the square were very impressive; I have never seen anything like it and don't believe there a place anywhere else like it. The guards looked very good in their uniforms.

The bus ride back to town was very hot, crowded and miserable. When we got to our stop Sonja and I were able to get off, but Claudia and Julia could not get off. We hurried to get to the next bus stop to reunite with them. When we got to our hotel, Sonja and I wanted to rest and take a nap while Claudia and Julia wanted to go to the bank and do more shopping.

When they returned they told us they had found a nice restaurant we could get some dinner if we get there in fifteen minutes. It's always a problem if you want to eat dinner early because the restaurants close about 2:30 and open at 7:00 p.m. for dinner. The owner of this restaurant was extremely nice to us, even though he was closed and having his own meal, he served us at the same time. The restaurant was beautiful. It was called Ristorante da Nazzareno Roma. The food was delicious and expensive. We enjoyed a bottle of Vino with our meal, had dessert and a small glass of liquor, compliments from the owner. He gave us free post cards. We were happy as we rushed back to the hotel, gathered our bags and headed for the train station. Lucky for us we were very close to the train station. We had more to bring back than we came with, and the bags were heavy.

When we arrived, the train was already there. The train system is very different than in the U.S. They have 1st class cars with compartments that seat six people. The seats can be pulled forward to face each other, so the person sitting opposite you can stretch their legs on your side and vice versa. It affords you enough comfort to be able to sleep if you are a good sleeper. It seemed that every half hour the express train would pass our train at a tremendous rate of speed, and the sound and air from that train generated so much noise it felt like we would be blown out of our compartment.

They also had 2nd class cars that seated eight people in each compartment. Going to Germany we had 2nd class tickets, which was ok until we changed in Venice; the train was full and we could not find a seat. Getting through the train, stepping over people with our heavy bags was a challenge.

We had met a nice young Italian man who asked to sit with us. After changing trains, we saw him again and followed him through the cars. There were no seats in 2nd class at all, so we found a car in 1st class with one Asian- looking man in it and decided we would pay the difference in the fare. We never had to pay the difference because the tickets were never checked. We nearly missed our stop in Innsbruck, Austria but Claudia woke us up in time.

We made a mad dash off the train. No one calls out the stops and we had to open the door of the train ourselves, which wasn't easy. We almost missed our stop when we came from Rome because the train was long, and we could not see the sign at the station. Claudia and Sonja stuck their heads out of the window and managed to see the sign. We each had an extra bag and had a very difficult time getting the door of the train open. Fortunately, I had seen someone else open the door and we managed to get out.

There were two young white males standing right near the door and they did not offer any assistance; only stared at us. We had to change trains four times going to Germany and Austria but coming from Rome we did not have to change.

After experiencing the train system, we got smart. When we boarded the train in Rome we found an empty compartment in first class and put bags on the two empty seats. We stretched our legs across the seats to make it appear that the whole compartment was taken. When it became dark we closed the door, pulled the curtains tight, and pretended to be sleeping, especially at one stop where there were lots of people boarding the train. They were all in the aisles and talking loudly. One young man came to our compartment and asked about a seat. We acted as if we did not understand English, so he went on.

It was very enjoyable being to ourselves. We had beer, soda, water and food. We arrived in Pordenone at 2 a.m. Tuesday morning, caught a cab at the station, dropped Sonja off at her house and continued to our hotel. Claudia and I kneeled and prayed to give thanks to God for a wonderful learning experience. We were so happy to be back safe. We took a shower and crashed.

It was August 4th and sleeping late was a pleasure. We managed to get moving about 10 a.m. The hotel restaurant was closed because it's Tuesday, but we managed to get coffee and tea before hiking to the Village. It was not easy. The streets were narrow, and no sidewalks were available. The people drive very fast, and there are many deep curves in the road. We had to cross from side to side depending on which side had the most space to walk, but it was fun. We told Sonja not to worry about us, we would walk and find food and we did. Not too far from our hotel we found a Café and Food Market. The lady at the food market could not speak English, but we managed to get what we wanted.

When we got back we enjoyed a delicious meal with a glass of wine; then we took a nap and enjoyed the rest of the day lounging. It rained and thundered quite a bit. Sonja came to check on us because she wasn't sure we had eaten. I asked God to bless her for being so sweet and loving, for taking time and doing everything possible to make sure we enjoyed our vacation. Later we made calls to check on everyone at home and found that all was well. The end of another perfect day.

On the morning of the 5th, I woke up early because of a nightmare. I got out of bed and wrote a letter to my friend Oliver, and a few post cards to others, before Claudia and

Julia woke up. The day was rainy and cool, but it didn't matter because we didn't have any plans. We decided to relax and do chores.

After breakfast I was experiencing some loneliness, so I called Oliver. He was happy to hear from me and it was nice to hear his voice. Claudia tried to call her son Ricky, but his line was busy. We sat in the hotel restaurant for a few hours and played a couple of records on the jukebox. When we heard Stevie Wonder singing, "I just called to say I love you", we all felt homesick. We quickly recovered after finding out we could catch a bus the next day outside our hotel, to get to the train station, to go to Pisa.

The possibility of shopping in Florence on the way home from Pisa really got Claudia excited, and also Julia. With plans in place, we had a relaxing afternoon. Sonja came after work to visit with us and I gave her a massage to relax some shoulder discomfort she was experiencing. Sonja's girlfriend and her husband came and joined us for dinner. We had a very delicious meal and really enjoyed our conversation.

We had a lot in common since the husband was from Philadelphia and the wife from Reading. We chatted, ate, and drank until late and everyone was tired. Our guests left, and we headed upstairs to retire. Julia remembered we needed to buy our bus tickets to Pordenone to catch the train. She had already undressed, so she put something on and went downstairs and purchased the tickets.

We got up early on the 6th and caught the bus in front of our hotel for Pordenone. When we arrived at the train station, our misinformation problems kicked in. We had thought that Pisa was a short trip, and we didn't expect the fare to be so expensive. Claudia was our negotiator. None of us could speak Italian (except a few words) but she could make the

Italians understand what she was trying to say. When the cashier gave her the total amount, she started to argue with him; as a result, we didn't get all the information we needed. I think if she had not upset the man he would have told us how long the trip was. We caught the train at 8:15 a.m., and it took us 6 ½ hours to get there, so everything we did was rushed.

After arriving so late we wanted to turn around and go back but thought it foolish to come so far and not see the Leaning Tower. Claudia bought more bus tickets to get to the Leaning Tower that we never used (same as in Rome), and we caught the first bus out. When we arrived the first thing was to get a cold drink. It was hot.

The Leaning Tower was spectacular! Everything, I thought it would be. After seeing it in books and the movies, seeing it personally and being able to go up inside of it was an unforgettable experience. We went almost to the top of the tower and looking out over the city was an indescribable moment in time. On the way up, I felt a little dizzy and had to hold on to the wall; after walking slower I was fine.

One young white girl passed out near the top in front of us, and I gave her companion some water and Claudia gave him tissues. It really helped because she came to after he put the water on her forehead. It was very hot and crowded on the way up to the top of the tower (the only downside), but the view was worth the effort. We were very fortunate to be able to go up inside of the tower because later I heard that people were not being allowed to go up because the structure was not considered safe. We went inside one of the Cathedrals inside the square near the Tower. Claudia and Julia lit a candle and prayed. I just prayed. It was very beautiful. At 5:45 p.m., we are on the train headed for home. This was turning out to be quite a day.

We changed trains in Firenze and had a hell of a time trying to find out what train to take next. When we did find out, we only had a few minutes to get on the train. Our next change was in Bologne, and we had to ask again what train to take. We changed again in Mestra. It was 12:20 a.m. and we were still on the train. We finally arrived in Pordenone at 12:40. We caught a cab and got to the hotel at 1:05, starved and exalted. We didn't have time to eat dinner in Pisa, so we got whatever we could on the train and other pit stops. It had been a very expensive day.

We met a nice English gentleman on the train to Pisa. He lived in London and worked in Italy. He told us the trains in London are much more expensive than in Italy. The airfare in Italy is outrageous, like over $200.00 for a half hour trip. More people in Germany speak English than in Italy. It is hard for the Italians to learn the English Language. They may know a little, but they shy away from speaking it.

We only encountered a few black people in our traveling but found out that the black women were not friendly at all. The men were just the opposite. Claudia asked a black woman about some collard greens at the open market and she pretended she didn't know what she was talking about. When we arrived back to our hotel from our long trip, we raided our refrigerator. Fortunately, we had food from our shopping in the village, and we ate it all. We had one can of sardines, two slices of ham, some cheese, one apple, one box of saltines, two or three slices of bread and one tomato. After eating we were happy to retire. We didn't have time to shop in Pisa but did get some post cards and I bought Sonja a scroll for her wall. A day well spent.

On August 7th Julia and I woke up at about 8:00 a.m. and it was raining. I was having a difficult time getting out of bed. I started to come alive after Julia went downstairs to the restaurant and got hot water for tea and coffee. Julia was smart and brought a hot water pot, tea bags, coffee, cream, cups and sugar. We were doing great until the pot blew out because the electricity in Italy is different, and we needed a transformer to use our stuff. Sonja brought hers over when she could, so we could do our hair. It was a heavy box that converts the electric to our usage. Sonja came on her lunch break and brought our groceries from the list we had given her the day before we left for Pisa.

Claudia and Julia went downstairs for breakfast and I stayed in bed. They brought me a bowl of hot vegetable soup. That was a great incentive to get me up and going, as I was in a deep sleep when they returned. The soup was delicious. Sonja also brought books that her friend Caroline had sent for us to read. Claudia devours books and she was deep into hers immediately while Julia and I were doing chores.

Sonja and her friend Aretha came and picked us up at about 7:00 p.m. for dinner at the Spaghetti House, which was one of our favorite restaurants in Aviano. It was crowded when we arrived, so we waited outside and took pictures. It was a family restaurant, and we were greeted by the owner. He was a very friendly man and we felt special from his jovial attitude and personality. The menu reminded me of a Ben & Jerry's Ice Cream menu, only spaghetti paired many ways. All the spaghetti was made on the premises, none from a box. You could choose spaghetti with seafood, vegetables, fish, scallops, shrimp, chicken, beef, pork, and other varieties. It was hard to choose but I decided to have mine with vegetables. We had a bottle of Vino of course. (I had never drunk so much wine in my life as I did in Italy.)

Drinking wine in Italy was as natural as drinking water. The wine was always paired with the meal, and it was perfect. I found the wine different than in the U.S.; it tasted better and did not make you feel bad. The Spaghetti House will remain in my memory as one of the best restaurants I have ever had the pleasure of eating in. It was not the most fabulous one, but the unique character and ambiance set it apart from other restaurants in my travels. After dinner we returned to our hotel and talked for a while before retiring. We were excited about going to Venice the next day.

It was not hard to get up early on the morning of August 8th; the excitement of going to Venice was enough. When Sonja came to get us, we were ready to go. We went to the cleaners to get our clothes and stopped at the BX to exchange some money. We went to the Burger King for sandwiches and to Sonja's house where we ate and relaxed a little before heading for the train station in Pordenone.

We caught the train for Venice around 2:00 p.m. It was a lovely sunshiny day, not too hot. When we arrived, the first thing was to get a cold drink and go to the bathroom. The first ladies room we found had an attendant sitting behind a cash register asking for 40 liters for us to use the toilet, so we decided to look further and found a public one that had the hole in the floor.

Those toilets were strange to me. I grew up in the country where we had out-houses, but we were able to sit down and do whatever you had to do. These toilets had no place to sit. You had to squat over the hole in the floor. I was so happy I did not have to use the toilet to do a bowel movement while traveling.

After relieving ourselves, we caught a boat ride to San Marco Square. I have always wanted to visit this place from the first time I ever saw it, either in the movies or on television. It was breathtaking and unbelievable; I could not believe my eyes. The boat ride to the square was awesome. After disembarking the boat, we walked to the San Marco Square. The sight of so many people and pigeons everywhere were just as I remembered from books and movies. A photographer in the square took pictures of us holding pigeons in our hands. The pigeons are very smart. They would come to you and eat out of your hand if they saw some corn; if they did not see the corn they would ignore you. We took pictures of each other, and after the pigeons ate all the corn we had it was time to leave.

We went on a walking tour and did some shopping until we were tired and hungry. We ate at an open restaurant that had the best French rolls that I had ever eaten in Italy. The Pizza was also delicious. We shopped a little more after eating and caught the boat back to the train station. It was dark at this time and we saw a line of gondolas in a procession. It looked as though it may have been a wedding party. They were singing and one of the gondolas in the center of the procession was decorated with flowers and lights. We took pictures of them.

One of the main things I wanted to do was to ride in the gondola, so we took a break from shopping and took a ride. The experience was beautiful and oh, so romantic, with a full moon in view. We started to sing "row, row, row your boat", and the Gondolier sang with us. We caught up with a group of other gondola's that had music and a soloist.
We were going down the river side by side, with the singing and music, and that made it very special. It would have been more romantic if we had our male companions with us, but we enjoyed the experience anyway. After finishing our boat ride, we went to a jewelry store and did more shopping. When we left the store, it was time to board the train to Pordenone. Sonja had left her car at the train station. We arrived back about 1:00 a.m. The uniqueness and beauty of the City of

Venice is like no other place in the world. I feel extremely blessed to have been able to visit this beautiful city twice in my life.

August 9th was our last day in Italy, and the weather was cloudy and cool. Sonja and her friend wanted to take us to Bar Trust Mountain for a cookout, but the weather was not conducive, and it was probably raining on the mountain. The second choice was to use the picnic area on the Air Force Base. This day started out with whatever can go wrong will. Sonja was supposed to pick us up around 11:00 a.m. She was always on time, except for this day. I thought something was wrong because it was after 12:00 noon when one of her friends drove her car to pick us up. When we arrived at her house we found that their friends, Max and Jerome, had left early to go somewhere, and Sonja didn't know where they went, or why they had to go someplace. Sonja was upset to say the least.

When they returned we found out that the brother of one of their friend had committed suicide and she had to go home to the U.S. Max and Jerome had taken her to the airport. Sonja drove by Aretha's house to see if she was coming with us, but she was not dressed. We packed up and headed for the picnic. The people with us were Calvin, Angie, Jerome, Slick and his wife, Sonja and Max. We forgot to bring paper plates and we needed some spray for the flies and bees, so Sonja and I went back to the hotel and stopped by the base on the way back.

The first obstacle was the train crossing, so we detoured. On the way to the hotel I realized that Claudia had the key to our room. We figured we could get in by asking the owner to let us in with their key, except the woman that was working at the time must have gone through a hundred keys and could not find the one to our room, so we could not get in.

On the way back, we stopped at the food market on the base and it had just closed. No paper plates and no bug spray today. We did go to the restroom in the hotel and that is all we accomplished before returning to the picnic. Angie was cooking, and some of the food was ready. It must have been about 5:00 p.m. now. The food was delicious and plentiful. We had the best shish-ka-bobs ever; and chicken, hamburgers, hot dogs, ribs, macaroni salad, baked beans, beer, liquor, wine and sodas.

On the picnic grounds were swings, sliding boards, monkey bars and seesaws. We had lots of fun acting like children. Claudia and I got on the seesaw but she was too lightweight to lift me up high, so we gave up on that. Claudia and Julia got on the swings and I climbed the monkey bars. After we did the children thing, we decided to relax and play cards. One of the couples invited us to their house after the picnic to see the movie "Cobra".

When Claudia and her group finished playing their last game we packed up and went to Slick's house. Their apartment was beautiful. They had furniture from Japan and the Philippines. Slick and his wife made us feel so welcome and comfortable; serving us popcorn and drinks during the movie was special. After the movie it was time to go home and start packing for our journey home the next day.

Sonja brought us back to the hotel and stayed with us to help settle our hotel bill. The owner was very nice and gave us a break on the nights that we stayed in Germany. We said our goodbyes to him shook hands and he gave us each a bottle of wine to take home. Our experience at this hotel was exceptional; we found the location, privacy, and the size to be perfect for ladies traveling alone. We always felt safe and were never intruded upon by anyone. The restaurant owner also gave us a beautiful poster menu from the restaurant printed in Italian. I had it framed when I returned home and hung it in my kitchen. It was a lovely reminder of our trip to Italy.

It was August 10th and time to leave Italy. We were up at 5:00 a.m. Sonja and her friend Caroline came to get us at 6:30. We needed two cars because of the luggage. We were off to Venice, which took about an hour. Only stopping to gas up and go to the bathroom, we got to the airport with time to spare. We took pictures and gave each other lots of hugs before checking in. It was open seating on the plane and we managed to be able to sit together.

Our first stop was in Rome. When we arrived, we discovered that our tickets showed that we were booked on stand-by. That was a shocker! Fortunately, the plane was not full. The three of us could not sit together, so Claudia and I sat in front of the wall where the movie screen was. It was very uncomfortable there because you cannot stretch your legs out unless you put them up on the wall.

Julia really had it bad! She was sandwiched in between two people and the person on the aisle seat was fat and hanging over her seat onto Julia's seat. Besides having difficulty getting up, she had packages in front of her. When I went back and saw Julia's situation, I became very pleased with mine. It was a long flight; eight hours and fifteen minutes to New York. I slept very little. Lucky for us Sonja's friend Caroline had given us some good books to read that helped a lot. We were happy to be back in the USA. Our experiences were exciting and will remain in our memories forever.

We were fortunate to get an early flight out of New York back to Philadelphia. When we arrived in New York, Julia and Claudia called home to inform everyone that we would be arriving early. One of Julia's friends picked us up in his van. When we got home, Julia's husband Frank had a delicious meal prepared for us. I had wanted Collard Greens ever since we arrived in Italy, and the only explanation I can think of is perhaps the country atmosphere that reminded me of home. We tried to find some, but I think the only people who planted them were Americans who planted them in their private gardens. They did not have them at the open market. We recognized some as we walked past some gardens.

Our welcome home dinner menu consisted of collard greens, fried chicken, cornbread, string beans, fresh sliced tomatoes and onions, potato salad, deep-dish apple pie and two cakes. The food was indescribably delicious! We all ate too much.

We all had some good times and ate some good food but no matter where you Rome or Roma there is no place like home! I thank God for a lovely daughter Sonja, who really went all out to show us a fabulous time.

God blessed us to see so much beauty and learn how other people live. It was a challenge and an interesting experience to have to change your money in many places. Most places did take the American dollar, but if you needed change you would be given their money. I wish that every American could travel to other countries. I believe it would change their attitude about the USA.

CHAPTER TEN

It Was a Grand Wedding!

You get to experience a lot in 74 years of living but being a Matron of Honor in my oldest sister's wedding was an experience I never thought would happen. My sister Claudia was 75 and had been a widow for 23 years, living at her home in Philadelphia. In February of 2000 her cousin, Lincoln Green, introduced her to a wonderful man named Stanley. He was age 78 and a widower for 15 years living in Ocean City, New Jersey. They were introduced at the Mayor's Ball in Pleasantville, New Jersey, and they spoke briefly, but there were no fireworks. It was not until a year later that Lincoln introduced them again at the same Mayor's Ball. This time Claudia had to remind Stanley that they had met the year before; he didn't remember until she mentioned something they talked about. At that moment something clicked in Stanley and they spent the rest of the evening dancing and talking. From that time, the love story began.

They kept in close touch via telephone, e-mail and commuting from Ocean City to Philadelphia to Sarasota, Florida. They also vacationed together, where their travels took them to France, Egypt, Bahamas, Puerto Rico, Las Vegas and many other places. During this period of seven years Claudia was given a beautiful diamond ring that was uniquely designed; it was unlike a traditional engagement ring and that had everyone guessing - is it an engagement ring? As time went by everyone was asking when are you two getting married? The answers were varied and elusive for a long time. Then suddenly at a candlelight dinner at his condo in Sarasota the date was set. There was a short time period, of approximately two and one-half months, to plan a wedding but everyone was excited to hear the news.

I have six daughters and they are very fond of their aunt Claudia, but when she said she wanted all six of them and her granddaughter Taylor in her wedding, they thought she was joking. She was not joking and we all got busy and made it happen. It was truly a family affair. A total of eighteen family members of the bride and groom were in the bridal party.

Before getting married the bride should have a shower, so that's what we did. Soliciting the help of my daughters, I managed to give Claudia a wedding shower that we will always remember, and she will never forget. As a keepsake we gave her a picture album filled with photos of her with each guest, each with a handwritten bit of advice for the bride.

As Claudia was opening her presents, my daughter Tauheedah was secretly writing everything that Claudia said about each gift. When she was done, my daughter said, "Okay this is what Claudia will say on her wedding night," and she proceeded to read the comments: "Ohh this is beautiful, I never had anything like this before, finally I have something decent, this is perfect and feels great!" Other things were said also, too numerous to mention. The laughter went on and on.

On the day of the wedding, the hairdresser (Claudia's niece Deanne), the make-up artist and the photographer came to her house early and made sure her hair, make-up and pictures were in order. The wedding party colors were reminders of autumn leaves and they blended with her gorgeous gown of satin champagne. When the limousine picked up the bridal party it had started to drizzle, but fortunately it was not a cold rain. We managed to get inside the church without getting wet.

The wedding was held in the beautiful Mt. Airy Presbyterian Church at Germantown Avenue and Mt. Pleasant Streets in Philadelphia. The program was simply regal; one guest referred to them as a King and Queen. After the prelude, the Lighting of the Family Candles was performed by the granddaughter of the groom and the grandson of the bride, and "Ave Maria" was performed by the flutist. The bridal party entered with the song "Holy" performed by the choir and the bride entered on the arm of her oldest son, Derrick.

The Call to Worship was given by the Pastor and the Statement on the Gift of Marriage was given while the bride, groom and bridal party were seated facing the minister. The families of the bride and groom were asked to stand in Affirmation of their support of this marriage, after which the congregation was asked to Affirm their support by standing. The anthem "Pavane" in the Renaissance style, was performed by the harpist. Prayer was rendered, and scripture was read by the bride's niece Deborah (1 Corinthians 13:1-13), and the groom's son Stanley Jr. (Colossians 3:12-17).

The rest of the program proceeded as follows: Anthem, "Embraceable You", Meditation (the bridal party standing), Vows, Exchange of Rings, Anthem "Marelles No. 7", Lighting of the Unity Candle, Prayer, Announcement of Marriage, Charge (Proverbs 3:3-6) read by cousin of the bride, Lincoln Blessing, and Recessional: "O Happy Day" by the choir.

Since this was my first time participating in a bridal party, I was astonished at the amount of work and the cost involved in having a large wedding. The bride and groom wanted to invite all their close family and friends, but it was impossible, so they had to cut their list to fit the size of the church and the number of people the venue would accommodate. After adding and eliminating several times they wound up with a list of one hundred sixty-five.

The church Sanctuary was used for the wedding and the lower level was used for hors-d'oeuvres and drinks. A video of the bride and groom's extensive travels was shown on that level. In the basement level the dinner was served.

While the church is old and beautiful the basement needed a lot of attention, and attention was what it got to the utmost. The event planners transformed the basement into a five-star restaurant area. Beautiful material covered the walls, trees and flowers were coming out of the floor. Enlarged pictures of the bride and groom were hung on the walls portraying them in the various countries they have traveled. It was simply beautiful! The waiters were first class and the food was excellent.

The bride and groom traveled from Ocean City to Virginia to catch the Auto Train and begin their 17-day honeymoon journey. They flew from Sarasota to Miami, from Miami to Rio de Janeiro where they stayed for three days before boarding the Princess Cruise Ship. The cruise took them to Montevideo in Uruguay, Buenos Aires in Argentina, the Falkland Islands, around Cape Horn to Ushuaia to Punta Arenus and Valparaiso and Santiago in Chile. After the cruise they flew back to Miami to return home to Sarasota.

Love can come at any age; keep your heart and mind open with a positive attitude. We do not know what God has in store for us, but we know that each day is a gift, and we should live it to the utmost, never taking things and people that we meet for granted. Stay in the present because the past has no power over the blessings that God has in store for you right now.

For anyone who is planning to be in a bridal party take my advice and wear comfortable shoes. You will be very glad you did.

Believing in Miracles

On September 17, 2007 at about 9:30 a.m. I was rushing to the Abington Hospital to be with my daughter, Deanne, who was scheduled to have a caesarian operation starting about 10:00 a.m. She called me from her cell phone and asked, "Where are you? I am just about to go to surgery." I told her that I was about halfway there, and I would be there shortly. It turned out that when I got there, she had been taken to the operating room. I was very disappointed that I didn't make it in time because she seemed as though she needed me to be there. Her husband Perry, daughter Victoria (4 yrs. old), and father-in-law Frederick were already there.

Perry was in the delivery room with her. He noticed that she was in distress and spoke to the doctor. The doctor immediately rushed him out of the room. They instituted a code blue, and doctors came running! Perry came to the waiting room and informed me and his father that something went wrong. He said they had put him out and would not tell him anything at that time. Sometime later, we were told that the baby was fine, and we could see him in the nursery. We were very excited about Parrish Joshua who weighed 6 lbs. 14 ounces, healthy and beautiful with a head full of hair. We were told that Deanne was in recovery.

Finally, the doctor told Perry he could come to see his wife. The fact that she was in ICU was scary. When he returned from seeing her the look on his face was indescribable. I knew something had gone very wrong. He told me to come with him and he walked me to the ICU. When I walked into the room I was shocked to see Deanne in a coma and her body was swollen all over. She had a breathing tube and other tubes attached all over her body. I was feeling guilty that I was late and didn't get to see her before they took her to surgery. "Now what", was my thought. I walked over to her and held her hand. I had been praying all day and continued to pray. I didn't know whether she could hear me, but I told her, "I am sorry for being late getting to the hospital." I told her that God would take care of her and she would be alright.

The nurses in attendance explained to me what had happened. During the operation she developed an amniotic fluid embolism; a catastrophic condition which can occur during pregnancy or shortly after delivery. The incidence in the United States is estimated only at 1 in 20,000 to 1 in 30,000 deliveries.

The likelihood of survival is nothing short of a miracle. The maternal mortality rate is 30 to 90 percent, and many survivors suffer irreversible neurologic sequelae caused by cerebral hypoxia. In other words, she stopped breathing and the blood from the fluid went into her veins. The doctor gave her CPR for several minutes, some said 12 to 15 minutes before she started breathing again and was put on a breathing machine. She had transfusions to replace the blood.

I called her five sisters and other family members. They left their jobs immediately and by nightfall they were all at the hospital. Out of the five sisters, Tauheedah was a registered nurse before becoming a doctor, and she was in Seattle. She left on the first flight she could get and arrived at the hospital early in the morning. Her expertise was so valuable to Deanne's treatment and recovery.

It seemed that one of the doctors resented the fact that Tauheedah expressed her opinion about Deanne's treatment. She did not always agree with them, but they respected her wishes. We all practically lived at the hospital for seven days, taking turns at staying overnight. Deanne was in a coma for three days, and the fourth day she woke up.

She did not know she had a baby and could not remember very much. On the sixth day she was moved to the maternity floor. She was blessed to begin breastfeeding also. Her memory was slowly returning. Deanne came home from the hospital on the ninth day (Oct. 8). I moved into her house that day to help Perry. She was in extreme pain and could not do much more than breastfeed the baby. Perry and I had a big job; getting Victoria ready for daycare, helping with homework, cooking and washing, fixing formula for the baby and so on. The breast milk was not enough, and Parrish had to have formula also.

During it all Deanne developed more pain from an infection and had to return to the hospital, but she was able to come home after four days. Although she was still in pain, it was much better. During the week Deanne returned to the hospital, her father-in-law, Frederick Hale, was hospitalized. Perry was going from one hospital to another. Frederick was fortunate to be at the hospital to see his grandson. He was a devoted grandfather and spent a lot of time helping with Victoria, picking her up from daycare most of the time, and keeping her on weekends. Mrs. Hale passed in 2004 when Victoria was a baby.

The Power of Prayer! During a brief period when I was at home, I called my Pastor, Rev. Williams, and asked for prayer for Deanne. He was out of town but called in a short time and prayed with me. He also told me to call his wife Connie, because she had a Prayer Team on the Internet. I called her, and she e-mailed the Prayer Team that same day. The next day I had e-mails coming from all over informing me that they were praying for Deanne. Deanne was a member of Enon at that time, and her Pastor, Rev. Waller and his congregation were praying also. I could say a lot more but will end by saying that God answers prayer! I moved back home on October 28th. Deanne and her family were doing

fine, and she prepared to open her new Beauty Salon
"Collage", at 6813 Germantown Avenue.

*James 5:16 Confess your faults one to another, and pray one
for another, that ye may be healed. The effectual fervent prayer
of a righteous man availeth much.* (KJV)

Forgiveness

I pray for God's mercy to allow me to not hold un-forgiveness
in my heart. It is like a cancer that eats away at your spirit
and keeps you from being a free loving person. The kind of
love that our God wants us to have toward one another;
Agape Love.

My daughter Deanne talked to me about forgiveness. Per our
religious belief, we must forgive people who hurt us and treat
us badly, so God will forgive us. She told me I needed to call
everyone that I was holding un-forgiveness toward and tell
them about it and forgive them. That was quite a lot for me to
do. It took me over a year to finally do that. I called several
family members. The thing about holding un-forgiveness is
that people don't know what you are holding against them
and they either don't remember or lie about it, so the only
person that is hurting is you. Some family members said they
could not remember or they remembered it a different way
than I did. I felt free of the hurt and pain after I released it
and forgave the people involved.

A devastating experience involving sex happened before I left
Gosport and moved to Philadelphia. It was very painful, and I
buried it deep inside. I forgot about it for years. I did not
want to cause any problems for Mama. I did not care about
the culprit, but I knew the pain and potential harm it would
create within the family. After I had downsized from my home
and moved to Delaware, I was reading a book in my office

that told of a young lady being raped by her master. I experienced an outburst that was uncontrollable, and I began to scream at the man and cry out loud as he took advantage of the female. All my experience that I had buried so deep inside, and tried to forget, came to the surface. I felt some relief from admitting it to myself but still could not talk about it to anyone else.

On this day, Mama and her children had left, and I thought I was home alone, casually going about my business getting ready for school. Suddenly, I was grabbed from behind and lifted off my feet and taken to the bedroom, which was a short distance from where I was standing, in the hall outside of the bedroom. I was literally thrown on the bed while kicking and screaming. I fought hard to resist but was overpowered by this grown man. I didn't know at that time that what happened to me was called rape, but I knew for sure I was not in agreement and it wasn't about a pair of shoes. I felt so dirty and guilty at the same time.

Did I bring this on myself? Did my consent for a pair of shoes cause this to happen to me? No! No! No! I was fully taken advantage of in each case by an adult male. I felt so dirty and worthless. The first encounter was about a pair of shoes that I agreed to and the second was ten times worse because I was not in agreement with it. After the incident, I washed myself and got ready and rushed to school with red eyes from crying. I thought the teacher would ask me why I was late and why my eyes were red. She did not notice and did not ask me any questions. I was angry with her because I thought she should have noticed something was wrong with me. I think if she had questioned me I would not have kept this secret for over 50 years.

I called the culprit to talk about what he did, and he tried to deny that it was rape and said he thought that there was mutual consent. I can't even explain how that hurt. I started screaming at him and crying. It gave me some relief to talk about what happened to someone even though it was the person who committed the act. I told him that I forgave him for what he did. He asked me for forgiveness as well.

If I ever see him again and can look him in the face without feeling that overwhelming swelling feeling of anger arise within me, I will know that I have forgiven him for sure. Right now, I am grateful for the peace I feel within my spirit.

Ephesians 4:32 And be ye kind one to another, tenderhearted, forgiving one another, even as God for Christ's sake hath forgiven you.

Conclusion

God saved me from being at the wrong place at the wrong time. I am referring to the five times our place of business was robbed – I was not there.

Every morning that I open my eyes to a new day I thank God, through prayer, reading scripture, and meditating on His Word. Time is precious, and I spend it learning new things, connecting with people, and helping whomever I can. Each breath I take is important and meaningful. I feel connected to the universe that God created and everybody and everything in it. I have a tremendous appreciation for the sunshine, rain, snow, trees, flowers, grass, birds, bees, insects and animals. All of God's Creation is special and important. I love when I can testify to the goodness of God to others, and I try not to miss an opportunity.

Reciting poems gives me much joy and I thank God for allowing me to share poems that are special to me like "The Creation", by James Weldon Johnson. God has blessed me to live 83 years and allowed me to grow mentally, spiritually, and in all areas that have resulted in a place of peace and joy! Even having loved and lost, it doesn't matter because God is still with me and guides me daily as I continue to grow in my relationship with Him.

The Lorene Bronner that started this story approximately ten years ago, God has redeemed from the strongholds of un-forgiveness, vanity, meanness, thinking more highly of myself than who I am. Freedom and peace of mind are mine when learning to love others the way that God loves me. Releasing those negative emotions and embracing new positive ones is inexplicable, and the results are remarkable. Many lessons have been learned on this journey, for example, helping others will bring help, apologizing when I am wrong will relieve me from stress.

From writing my story God made it possible for me to peel away layers of pain that plagued me for many years. My hope is that others who read my story will be helped by it and be able to avoid the pitfalls that I have experienced. Having taken a close look inside of myself revealed some things that I did not like or want to share but seeking to find my truth led me to confess those parts of my personality that I don't like and still making great strides to change as I continue to grow in faith.

If you have taken time to read my story, I hope you have been inspired to become a better you. God made us all special and gave us gifts. What we do with our gifts is up to us, because He also gave us choices. The sacrifices that I have made for my family were not in vain, and God allowed me to live to experience ten-fold the love I gave in return daily.

God made each person unique and different; we all have a different fingerprint. He gave us talents to share with others.

My desire is to discover all my gifts and use them to glorify God and help other people. We should love ourselves and not try to be like someone else. Appreciate the You that God made and be the best person you can be.

Matthew 6:33 But seek ye first the kingdom of God and his righteousness; and all these things will be added unto you.

APPENDIX

Daughter # 1: Deborah

Deborah attended Spelman College in Atlanta, GA; Chaminade University, Honolulu, Hawaii; and graduated with Bachelor of Business Administration degree from Temple University in Philadelphia, PA. She served in the US Army, 25th Infantry Division, Schofield Barracks, Hawaii for three years. Deborah worked for the Dept. of Justice, Federal Bureau of Prisons; the Dept. of the Navy, Human Resources Services Center Northeast and the Office of Personnel Management, Staff Acquisition, Human Resources Solutions, for a total of thirty years and seven months in the Human Resources field. She is now retired and enjoying life.

Deborah gave birth to two sons. Although her first son died within days of being born, her second son served in the Marine Corps and is currently on active duty in the US Army and close to retirement. Her daughter-in-law served in the US Air Force and is currently serving in the Air National Guard while performing research for her Ph.D. Deborah's granddaughter is on a State traveling soccer team while attending elementary school.

Daughter # 2: Kala

Kala loves to cook, bake cakes and entertain friends and family. She has been a member of a pinochle club for over 30 years. She began working for the Federal Government at the age of 16 while attending Northeast High School and continued after graduation. Kala retired from the position of Management Analyst in July 2015 with over 40 years of service. During her career, she was an administrative assistant for three Military Generals and received numerous meritorious awards for outstanding service. Kala is a member of the Nazarene Baptist Church and she has served on the Board of Trustees for over eleven years. She was also an Aerobics Instructor for over ten years.

She became a caregiver for family and friends in 2010 and continues this journey today. She is a loving, caring mother of her son Donald Austin who was born with Down Syndrome in 1978. The doctors said he probably would not live to become an adult and suggested that he be placed in a facility. Donald was very sick during his early childhood, but because of the loving care he received from his mother and family, Donald celebrated his 39th Birthday on July 14, 2017 at Disney World in Orlando, Florida.

Dr. Tauheedah Bronner is a seasoned healthcare professional with over 35 years of experience. She has a diverse background in the clinical, business and technical healthcare settings. For the past 15 years she has assumed various roles in the product development and implementation of healthcare IT solutions. Prior to that, she practiced as a registered nurse in the managed care environment in the areas of utilization review, case, disease, and population health management. She started her career in cardiovascular ICU nursing, practicing in the clinical setting for ten years.

Most recently, Tauheedah decided to follow her passion and love for holistic, natural medicine returning to school to achieve a four-year doctorate in Naturopathic Medicine from the University of Bridgeport in Connecticut, graduating in 2013. She is a licensed Naturopathic Physician in the state of Maryland, and a licensed Registered Nurse in the state of Pennsylvania. Dr. Bronner is also a Certified Professional of the Academy of Healthcare Management, American Association of Health Plans and the BCBS Association. She received her undergraduate bachelor's Degree in Nursing from West Chester University in Pennsylvania in 1980.

Deanne has been a seasoned professional in the beauty industry for the past 36 years. She is a Licensed Cosmetologist, teacher and business entrepreneur. Deanne is the owner of Collage Hair Studio in Mt. Airy, Pennsylvania, and has successfully been in business for over ten years. Deanne is a devoted mother, wife and grandmother. She gave birth to four children, including three sons and one beautiful daughter. She has one granddaughter. Deanne is an ordained Deaconess at Covenant House of God Church and carries the position of Armor Bearer to her Apostle.

Daughter # 5: Linda

Linda has 33 years of service with the Federal Government. She is a Contract Specialist at the Department of Defense. Linda has a bachelor's Degree and a master's Degree in Business Administration from La Salle University in Philadelphia. Linda is also a member of Delta Sigma Theta Sorority. She is the proud mother of two sons and she has one granddaughter. Linda is a faithful member of the Enon Tabernacle Baptist Church and serves on her favorite ministry for helping homeless children.

Daughter # 6: Lorene Lolita

Lorene Lolita was Linda's Twin and they were the first and only set of twins born to Charles and Lorene Bronner. Shortly after birth, Lolita sorrowfully did not survive.

As a little girl, Sonja's biggest dream was to travel around the world. She embarked on her path by joining the U.S. Air Force active duty at age 19. Sonja holds a Bachelor of Science Degree in Business Administration from La Salle University and a Master of Science in Administration Degree from Central Michigan University. Additionally, she achieved two certifications in Logistics. Though she changed careers a few times she never veered from her goal to see as many countries as possible. Today, Sonja has been to Europe, East and West Africa, the Persian Gulf, Western Asia and at least 15 islands in the Caribbean and North America. Sonja transitioned from her military career to work for our cousins, owners of Bronner Brothers Inc. Some of her accomplishments are mentioned earlier in the book.

Today, Sonja is a Logistician for the Federal Government at the Defense Logistics Agency Troop Support. Whenever the opportunity arises, she mentors and coaches' others to reach their goals and aspirations personally and professionally.

One of her hobbies is writing poetry. She has given spoken word performances while overseas and, in the U.S., expressing her passion to encourage others to reach their greatest potential. Sonja's desire to give back to her community is always at the forefront of her life. She created "Women at the Cross" ministry as an opportunity to have Bible study and conversation about our Lord and Savior Jesus Christ with women around the world. She has spent many years praying for others and giving of her various resources to support men and women who are in transition.

ABOUT THE AUTHOR
Lorene Bronner

I was born in Gosport, Alabama in Clarke County, on May 11, 1934. My mother gave birth in her father's house, attended by a midwife. Early childhood was spent in Gosport and Mobile, Alabama, where I attended elementary and began high school. My family moved to Philadelphia when I was age sixteen and I graduated from William Penn High School for Girls located at 15th & Wallace Streets. I also attended Temple University for a couple of years. Later, I attended Hystyle School of Cosmetology and received a license to practice in a Beauty Salon.

My work in a beauty salon was not my passion, and I discontinued the practice after about two years and continued my education at Temple University taking computer classes. I became certified as Stenographer-11 from classes taken at the Opportunities Industrialization Center (OIC). Learning is not a destination for me; it is a continuing process on this journey and I never miss an opportunity to learn something new. I am currently involved in three Bible Study groups.

I met the love of my life in 1950 when I moved from Alabama to Philadelphia. We dated five years before marriage and became the parents of seven girls. We owned and operated Bronner's Lounge, a bar business in West Philadelphia for eight of our 23 years of marriage.

I lived in my home in West Oak Lane on Grange Street for 45 years before moving to an apartment for four years and then to Newark, DE with my third oldest daughter. After selling Bronner's Lounge, I became employed as secretary to Dr. James L. Dandridge, Pastor of Mt. Pisgah A.M.E. Church and remained the secretary under Dr. Mickarl Thomas until I retired after 20 years of service. During that same period, I worked two other part-time jobs; sales manager for the World Book Encyclopedia Company, and salesperson for the Bronner's Brothers Hair Care Products Company and Upscale Magazine.

Many years of my life have been spent as a community and civic activist, serving as secretary to the 1400 Grange Street Block Club for ten years. I have many proud memories of our accomplishments, working together to keep our neighborhood drug-free and beautified. I have also been a member of the Nazarene Baptist Church family for 47 years, singing in the Senior Choir for 30 years, participating in the

Widow's Group at Nazarene for 10 years, attending Sunday School and participating in various programs.

My life has been enhanced greatly by the connections I have with the Widows of King David Lodge #52. I was instrumental in forming a Widow's Group in 1989 after being taken to dinner by the Lodge Brothers in 1985. With the assistance of my Sister-in-Christ, Alice Baker, we started a newsletter that is still progressing after 28 years. This is a labor of love and I receive tremendous satisfaction from it. The Lodge Brothers are in their 33rd year of taking us to dinner.

I Am Growing in Faith!!

Portraits by Earle Brown
Eyes of Distinction
Photography & Creative Arts

In Honor of Sonja Jean Bronner
1966 – 2018

Lorene Bronner is moving forward and publishing her life story in honor of her daughter Sonja, knowing that Sonja would want it to be so. She was very excited to see the book completed and so, with love, it is published.

The stories of life so truthfully told in this book are in the past and Lorene now faces a new time of challenges, one that God has chosen. Since the book was completed prior to Sonja's transition, it seems appropriate to let readers know that Lorene is still strong and Growing in Faith. We thank her for putting more love into the world.

Ida Lawrence, Editor
May, 2018

Miss Me But Let Me Go

When I come to the end of the road
And the sun has set for me
I want no rites in a gloom-filled room.
Why cry for a soul set free?

Miss me a little but not too long
And not with your head bowed low.
Remember the love that once we shared,
Miss me but let me go.

Author Unknown

Made in the USA
Middletown, DE
14 February 2019